The Art of Catching

The Secrets and Techniques of Baseball's Most Demanding Position

The Art of Catching

The Secrets and Techniques of Baseball's
Most Demanding Position

Brent Mayne

Cleanline Books
Costa Mesa, California

3rd printing 2013

ISBN 978-0-9815386-5-5 (softcover)
ISBN 978-0-9815386-4-8 (ebook)
LCCN 2008921835

ATTENTION CORPORATIONS, UNIVERSITIES, COLLEGES, AND PROFESSIONAL ORGANIZA-TIONS: Quantity discounts are available on bulk purchases of this book for educational, gift purposes, or as premiums for increasing magazine subscriptions or renewals. Special books or book excerpts can also be created to fit specific needs. For information, please contact Cleanline Books, 2701 Harbor Blvd., E-2, #203, Costa Mesa, CA 92626.

Contents

Introduction

"Two hundred million Americans, and there ain't two good catchers among 'em."

—CASEY STENGEL

When asked about the shortage of quality catching, American League manager Ralph Houk replied, "There's a great opportunity for boys who want to catch in pro ball today." The odd thing is this comment was made fifty years ago, but it's just as relevant now as then. Why shouldn't you be the next person to take advantage of this situation to excel on your Little League team, earn a college scholarship, or even play in the big leagues? Someone has got to do it. It could be you.

This book gives you the most cutting-edge information ever presented on the art of catching. I'm passing on the secrets that allowed me to enjoy a fifteen-year major-league career and that will help you excel as a catcher or a catching instructor. I demystify the catching position and make the point clear that if I could do it, you can too. How am I so sure? I have been to the top of the mountain, playing with or against the best in the world, and I will tell you from experience there is plenty of room up there if you can *just play solid defense*. The techniques I show you, if practiced until they become second nature, will allow you to get the most out of your God-given talent and maximize your potential.

Another great thing about this information is that it's applicable to the youngest Little Leaguer all the way up to the oldest veteran in the big leagues...and everyone in between. In other words, these fundamentals are basic enough for an eight-year-old to grasp and apply but powerful enough to allow an athlete to excel at the big-league level. These simple ideas, founded on athletic truths, will make you a better player or coach.

Time for a Change

I am constantly amazed at the lack of quality information available to those interested in catching. The thing is, baseball has been dissected and taught from every angle. Every library offers great wisdom for aspiring hitters, infielders, pitchers, and outfielders. Expert coaching on these subjects is everywhere. Catching has no such treasure trove of information, and that is why so many people teach catching incorrectly; most of the time, they don't teach it at all. I am not just talking about the Little League level. I am referring to the lack of informed coaching from Little League all the way up to the big leagues. After spending fifteen-plus years at the highest level of baseball and crossing paths with countless coaches and managers, I can tell you there is but a handful of people able to articulate the art of catching.

Most of the information being taught is still from the Johnny Bench era. Although I acknowledge his greatness and contributions to the game, this style of catching is from the 1970s and severely outdated. Gone are the days when the majority of pitchers throw the ball in the 80–85 mph range. Today everything has sped up to the point where everybody throws 90–100 mph—with movement! This type of speed demands a different approach if one is to be consistently successful. This type of speed demands mobility and focus like never before.

Baseball is crying out for good catchers. It is the most critical defensive position on the field—who else gets to touch the ball just about every time it moves? It is the focal point of the infield, a lot of fun, and by far the easiest way to score a college scholarship or have a big- league career, even if you are not a great athlete.

It's my belief that the simple ideas in this book will pick up the subject, dust it off, and propel us into the future. I hope this information will provide you with a template to be a better player or coach and have more fun doing it. No longer are we just going to pick the biggest, most un-athletic kid and slap the gear on him! It's time to learn the art of catching. Good luck, have fun, and get after it.

Chapter 1

History

"It's a haunted game in which every player is measured against the ghosts of all those who have gone before."
—KEN BURNS

Let me start at the beginning by giving you a brief history of catching styles and telling you a bit about my background. An in-depth history of the position and the equipment would be interesting but is beyond the scope of this book. I do think it's important,

"We used no mattress on our hands,
No cage upon our face;
We stood right up and caught the ball,
With courage and grace."
—GEORGE ELLARD, 1869 RED STOCKINGS

however, to understand the evolution of the catching glove because advances in its form have paved the road for catchers to change and improve their techniques.

The Glove

It all started sometime around the 1890s when a couple of ballplayers by the names of Joe Gunson and Harry Decker had a hand in inventing the catcher's glove. This thing took on the look of a small, round pillow without webbing or lacing. Improvements were made in the late 1930s by Harry Latina, who worked for the Rawlings company, helping to usher in catching's glory years. Between 1931 and 1937, there were six future Hall of Famers catching for their teams at the same time! Players like Gabby Hartnett, Ernie Lombardi, Mickey Cochrane, Rick Ferrell, and Bill Dickey brought a combination of offensive and defensive prowess that has yet to be equaled in any era.

Gabby Hartnett

Ernie Lombardi

Mickey Cochrane

Rick Ferrell

Bill Dickey

Yogi Berra

Roy Campanella

Baseball fans of the 1950s enjoyed the styles of two more great catchers, Yogi Berra and Roy Campanella. Because advances in the glove remained static, these Hall of Famers still had to use two hands to catch the ball. Why do I mention this? Among other things, having to use two hands requires an upright type of squat and is extremely hazardous. This is why, if you ever have the pleasure of meeting receivers from the pre-1960s era, you will notice errant balls have caused their fingers to point in every direction but normal. Shaking hands with them can be a challenge. These guys were tough, and I am not sure, but I think the term "tools of ignorance" was probably coined around this time.

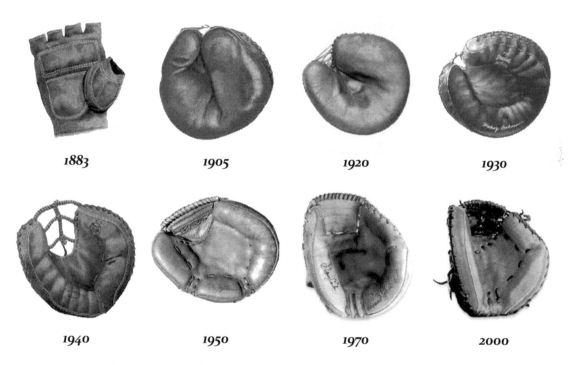

1883   1905   1920   1930

1940   1950   1970   2000

Although this early glove had a pocket, it had no breaks and required two hands to catch the ball so it wouldn't pop out. That, and the fact that the strike zone was much higher than today, gave catchers from that era a distinctive look. Many of them caught in a semi-crouch with both palms facing the pitcher in anticipation. When I see photos from this time, a couple of things generally come to mind. First, they look like they are just asking for a foul ball in the crotch. Second, it appears to me that their posture is fairly athletic, despite (or maybe because of) the semi-crouch. You will see what I mean when I expand on that thought later.

Hall of Famer Roger Bresnahan demonstrating the upright stance common to catchers of the early 1900s.

Another good image showing turn of the century catching style.

So fast-forward to the late '60s when players like Randy Hundley and later Johnny Bench helped the glove evolve into basically the shape it has today. Taking their cue from the flexible hinges and long oval-shaped pockets of first basemen's gloves from the 1950s, these guys revolutionized catching technique by using a glove that snapped closed on contact with the ball, essentially letting them work with only one hand. This eliminated the risk of exposing their bare hand, made it possible to receive the ball more consistently, and had the added bonus of saving their fingers. Meanwhile, the strike zone got lower, catchers squatted deeper, and the modern era of catching was born. Standouts from this era include Thurman Munson, Ted Simmons, Carlton Fisk, Gary Carter, and Bob Boone. It is interesting to note, however, that since 1965 only three catchers have been inducted into the Hall of Fame: Bench, Carter, and Fisk.

Johnny Bench   *Gary Carter*   *Carlton Fisk*

Talk about a prolonged recession in the catching business! Even more surprising to me is the fact that since that era, we have seen no great advances in equipment or made any great strides in catching technique, even though the speed of the game has drastically increased.

How I Became a Catcher

Now, let me switch gears and take you out to Southern California, circa 1985. My father, Mike Mayne, was in the in the middle of a very successful twenty-year stint as the coach of the Orange Coast College baseball team. I was in the middle of a not-so-successful stint as the second baseman for the Costa Mesa High School Mustangs. The problem lay in the simple fact that I was too slow and too small. Colleges were not pounding the door down. It was decision time. Did I want to continue to play baseball, or was it time to focus on something out-side of sports? My father, understanding the great void of skilled catchers, ap-proached me and said he had an idea. He was honest and told me in so many words that my only chance of continuing on as a ballplayer involved strapping on the gear.

Serendipitously, at the same time I was changing positions, my father, Cal State Fullerton coach Larry Corrigan, and big-league receiver Jamie Nelson were involved in the process of breaking down the mechanics of catching and more or less reinventing it...and they needed a guinea pig for this experiment. They needed someone (preferably with no catching experience because there would be no bad habits to break) to see whether the "Bench style" could be

My father and I during my season at Orange Coast College.

improved upon with their innovative ideas about athletic foundation, stances, and receiving and blocking techniques. With my options severely limited, I jumped at the opportunity and quickly embodied their vision of a modern catcher. When all the dust settled, I ended up with a successful big-league career largely due to these teachings. To make a long story short, I believe the forward thinking of these men did nothing less than bring the catching position into the twenty-first century. To my way of thinking, they turned the position from one of sluggishness into one of the most dynamic on the field. Most of what I will be passing on to you finds its roots in their ideas and wouldn't exist without their insight and hard work.

Chapter 2

The Foundation

"Do not worry if you have built your castles in the air. They are where they should be. Now put the foundations under them."

—HENRY DAVID THOREAU

Before we dive into the specific fundamentals involved in catching, I would like for you to understand what I believe to be good athletic positioning. We have all heard the saying "don't

"The most solid stone in the structure is the lowest one in the foundation."

—KAHIL GIBRAN

build a house on a shaky foundation." Well, the same holds true for a catcher's base. Good athletic posture will provide the catcher with a solid foundation and provide him with an unchanging vantage point to remedy shortcomings by simply tracing the movement back to the point where his posture breaks down and it comes unstacked. In other words, when things are unraveling or you are unsure about something, first make sure your posture is athletic.

Before we establish the basis of a good athletic posture, let me ask you a question: Do you know what controls the balance in your body? If you said the inner ears, you would be right. Following that fact, it stands to reason that wherever your head goes, your body will follow. This is an important fact because when you boil it all down, successful athletics are basically about balance and power. A good athletic position, as I define it, is when all body parts are "stacked" one on top of the other. The head is stacked over the shoulders, which are over the trunk and hips, which in turn are stacked over the knees and feet. Like I said, it is a position of maximum power and balance.

Nolan Ryan stacked and delivering a pitch from a position of maximum power.

One sumo wrestler with a perpendicular back and solid athletic positioning. One sumo with a parallel back and out of balance.

Seemingly unrelated sports begin to look similar when you notice athleticism. Surfer Taj Burrow making a powerful move and looking a lot like Nolan Ryan.

Ben Hogan, one of the greatest golfers of all time, demonstrating the dynamic athleticism common to all elite athletes regardless of sport or era.

It is my belief that the world's greatest athletes, regardless of sport, more or less live in this position. To put it another way, the best athletes stay "stacked" longer and more often than the average athlete. Picture in your mind Muhammad Ali delivering a knockout punch or Tiger Woods pounding a 350-yard drive. Or imagine Michael Jordan dunking the ball or Barry Bonds

Ivan Rodriguez stacked and ready to deliver a powerful throw.

The parallel back, "Bench style" marked the 1970s but can still be seen with many modern-day catchers.

crushing a home run. Maybe you prefer Nolan Ryan delivering a 100 mph fastball or Ivan Rodriguez throwing out a base stealer by ten feet. You see, it doesn't matter whether you're talking about surfing, sumo wrestling, or playing baseball, consistent success depends on a solid foundation, and athleticism looks the same in all sports.

So this is where we begin our journey. It is very important to understand this concept because no matter what happens—what body type we have, how much flexibility we possess, a new technique that we are trying—we must put it up to the light and ask ourselves if we are in good athletic posture and able to stay stacked. For example, whenever I have a problem blocking the ball or find myself a half step behind the action, the first place I look is at my foundation. I make sure that every movement I make in the sequence is athletic.

Staying stacked defines the art of catching style and marks a major departure from the way receiving is traditionally taught. As we touched on before, lower strike zones

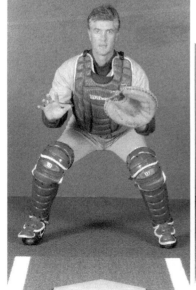

Turn-of-the-century stance, the "Bench-era" stance, and the "art-of-catching" stance.

and modern gloves have required deeper stances and enabled a one-handed catching style from receivers of the post-1960s era. This "Johnny Bench" style has the catcher in a position with his back parallel to the ground. Not only does this look exhausting and put a lot of pressure on the lower back, but it also fails to conform to the athletic position of balance and power. Remember, your balance is in your ears, and where your head goes, your body will follow. With your back parallel to the ground, your head is well in front of your body and your first movement will always be to fall forward. Your lateral movement is severely limited as is your ability to reach high pitches.

I would rather see your posture mimic that of an infielder fielding a ground ball. From a standing position simply bend your knees and squat down, being sure to keep your back fairly perpendicular to the ground. Your balance will be restored by squaring your head over your shoulders, which will be over your hips, and so forth. Automatically, you should feel more freedom because there won't be anything hindering your ability to move laterally. All things considered, this is a pretty comfortable squat, and with a little practice you should feel as if you could stay in it for nine innings. I find it funny that photos of the old-time catchers from the '30s and '40s show them to be in better athletic positions than many modern-day receivers! That is probably due to the semi-crouch and the more perpendicular back.

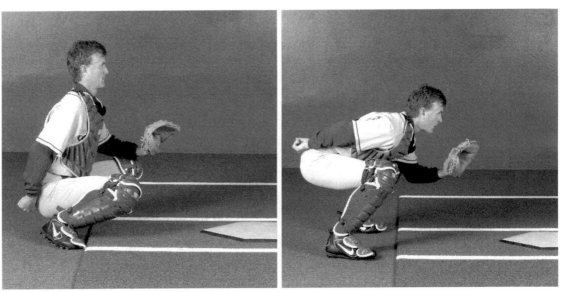

Perpendicular back vs. parallel back.
Which position looks more athletic, balanced, and comfortable?

I would like to mention that this is a very natural position and also very efficient and simple. As the game gets faster and faster, it is important that the catching position get simpler and simpler. Cut out any extra movements and streamline your actions. It can't get a whole lot more simple than just going into a full squat while keeping your back fairly straight. This body position is the foundation from which we will change the whole look of receivers from immobile lumps to dynamic and entertaining athletes.

Key Foundation Points

1. Regardless of your unique physiology, strive to have and keep a solid foundation throughout all your movements.

2. A solid foundation consists of your body parts staying stacked: head between shoulders, which are over your trunk and hips, which are in between your knees and feet.

3. Balance is in the ears. Where your head goes, your body will follow.

4. Try to adopt a stance that keeps your back fairly perpendicular to the ground, not hunched over or horizontal.

5. To correct a problem with any aspect of your game, break down the movements in slow motion and find the point where your posture becomes un-athletic.

Chapter 3

Stances

"There is no one correct way to bat, and so of course there is no one correct stance for it."

—STAN MUSIAL

L et us now get into the specific body positions of the catcher's stance. To the untrained eye, there would seem to be only one position for the receiver, but I find it more effective to teach three distinct stances to fit different situations. The first stance is the "sign stance" and is used to give your signals to the pitcher. The second is what I call the "comfort stance" or your most comfortable squatting position (keeping good athletic posture, of course). This stance is used when it is not important whether the ball stays in front of you. To be more specific, this is the position to use when there is no one on base and when there are fewer than two strikes. The third stance is the "blocking/throwing stance," used when a ball in the dirt needs to be blocked to prevent a runner from advancing or to keep a batter from getting to first on a wild third strike. This is also the most effective stance from which to throw out attempting base stealers. Having three stances may sound like overkill, but as you will see, they are all necessary to help the catcher adapt both mentally and physically to any situation. A reminder—these stances will look slightly different from person to person because everyone's body is different. Keep in mind the theory of staying stacked and the quote above from Stan Musial as you adapt your unique physiology to these positions.

Sign Stance, Cheaters, and Signals

The sign stance is the simplest of the three stances and is used to give the signals to the pitcher and shield opponents from stealing information. There are no rules against stealing signs, so it is the responsibility of the catcher to make sure it doesn't happen. There's a saying in baseball that goes, "If you are not cheating, you are not trying." This is said partially in jest, but to be honest, it's the plain truth. The next time you watch a pro ballgame, pay attention to the base runner leading off first as the camera cuts to him. If you look closely, you will notice that as he leads off, his gaze is often not on the pitcher but torqued about as far left as is possible. Guess what he is trying to do. That's right—he's looking into the catcher's crotch. The runner is trying to steal the signs, so he will know which pitch is coming (something slow like a curveball is obviously a better pitch to run on) or whether a pitchout or throw-over sign is being given. He either uses his peripheral vision or relies on the first base coach to alert him to a pick-off throw since he is not focused on the pitcher. If a right-hander is at bat, the runner may even choose to relay this pitch information to him! This is not even to mention the "cheating" that goes on from a runner on second base to the batter. As a hitter, I cannot tell you how much easier it is to hit a guy like Randy Johnson when you know what pitch is coming.

Keeping the pitches secret is also the reason why the first and third base coach's boxes are a decent distance from the baselines. If they were any closer, they would be getting the signs, too. Keep an eye on them and make sure they are actually within the confines of those boxes as nobody is above suspicion. And while we are on the subject, make sure that the hitter himself is not "peaking back" to get the signals—you would be surprised how many batters do this and are good at it. If you catch one, protocol calls for you to give him warning and threaten a ball under the chin if he doesn't respond. Pretty wild, isn't it? The games within the game. The point of all this isn't to scare you; it's just to urge you to pay attention. Keep it simple and just assume everyone is trying to get your signs. Since there are really no rules against stealing signs, and as Billy Martin once said, "Cheating is as much a part of the game as hot dogs and scorecards," it's important that you get into a good habit of protecting your signs like a poker player would protect his cards.

So now that I have you thoroughly paranoid, let's get back to the particulars of the sign stance. Standing with your feet about shoulder-width apart, toes parallel and directed toward centerfield, bend your knees into a full squat, making sure your back is fairly straight and your head is over your shoulders (not hunched over). The weight should be on the balls and toes of the feet, and the knees should point toward the pitcher. Keep your knees as closed and parallel as possible to prevent opponents from picking signs while at the same time allowing enough of a gap for the pitcher to see. The glove should be relaxed and hang down, shielding the third base coach from seeing anything.

Front and side views of the sign stance.
Notice the position of the hands and feet and how stacked the upper body stays.

When it comes to actually giving the signals with the hand, it's important to guard against revealing information. Giving the sign too low or high or excessive movement of the right elbow will reveal signs. From the squat, let the signal hand follow the inseam of the pants—easily falling into the crotch area to obtain proper height. The forearm should be relaxed and rest on the crease of the leg while the elbow stays close to the right hip. Be careful that your elbow doesn't bounce around when your hand makes different signs. Your arm should do the same thing no matter what number is being thrown down. People in the dugout and on-deck hitters love to watch that elbow for telltale signs.

I should also mention some solutions to the common problem of pitchers not being able to see the signs. The catcher is in a hard place trying to keep the signals between the battery, and shadows develop when the knees get too narrow. Add to that the fact that pitchers as a group don't see very well (a big reason they specialize in pitching and not hitting), and you have a problem. How many times have you seen a game grind to a snail's pace as a frustrated pitcher squints to get the sign and, not seeing it, calls the catcher out to get things straight? Fans get upset, infielders get upset, the manager gets really upset, and the game drags on. The solution? Know who can see and who can't beforehand and simply wrap some trainers tape around your sign fingers or paint your fingernails with whiteout. In a pinch, you can always drag the back of your hand on the chalk of the baseline to help bring some light to the situation. Problem solved—and that will close our discussion on the sign stance and all of its issues.

Comfort Stance

The comfort stance is the position you squat in when you do not need to block the ball. Basically, that means situations in which there are fewer than two strikes with no one on base. Your "comfort" takes priority in this situation, although you will still maintain a good athletic posture. This stance has no ideal or perfect position as everyone has a different physiology and different level of flexibility. I can tell you that it is mandatory that your upper body stay stacked regardless of your personal situation, and I share my own comfort stance as a guideline. I would also urge you to be patient and practice finding your balance in all of these positions. Many of them will be new and engage different muscles than you are accustomed to using, possibly resulting in initial soreness and discomfort. Take it slowly and figure out the best athletic squat for yourself.

There is a sequence I follow and recommend to everyone I coach. Right after giving the sign, make a good target, so the pitcher immediately has something to focus on. Then follow your target into the stance. So your sequence of getting into your setup, regardless of the situation, is always sign-target-stance.

My comfort stance goes something like this: From the sign stance, I give a target, then take a six- to eight-inch jab step with my right foot, then do the same with the left foot. (It is not important which foot goes first; it is usually determined by what side of the plate the pitch will be coming to.) My weight is distributed on my insteps, toes splayed and more or less pointing down the baselines. I keep my back straight, relaxed, and fairly perpendicular to the ground, making sure my head is back and over the balls of my feet. I constantly monitor my position as the game wears on, as I have a tendency to get tired and hunch over, losing my athletic posture.

It is extremely important that you give a consistently good target and keep your glove arm relaxed. With this in

Properly executed comfort stance with back fairly straight, head back, and glove hand relaxed on knee, providing a good target. Throwing hand is out of the way.

mind, let the forearm and elbow of the glove hand rest comfortably on the left leg and knee. To maximize the pitcher's focus area and to put you in good receiving position, give the target with fingers pointing toward the sky, as if you were waving hello to the pitcher. This can be tweaked slightly to the left or right in anticipation of ball movement (more on that later). Finally, since this isn't a throwing situation, keep your free hand behind your body—protected and out of the way.

One last observation and rant before we finish with the comfort stance: I go to ballgames or watch them on television for entertainment. Nothing bores me more than

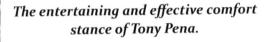

The entertaining and effective comfort stance of Tony Pena.

watching a lazy catcher or one who does the same thing all the time. This may be a little bit of a stretch, but could you imagine if you paid big bucks to see an entertainer in concert and all he or she did was stand there and sing? Entertainers get paid to move and perform, and I feel the catching position should be dynamic and exciting as well. With that in mind, I love it when I see a receiver who has multiple comfort stances. A guy who comes immediately to mind is Tony Pena. Whether or not you liked his style, you cannot deny his enthusiasm. He was anything but boring. I think that occasionally dropping a knee or extending a leg or doing something to provide the pitcher, the fan, or just yourself with a different look can be very engaging and effective. I am not talking about showing off. There is a difference between showing off and showmanship. I am pleading with you to practice a little showmanship. I am talking about bringing a little joy and lightness to the position. I am talking about taking your game to the next level. I want you to be both a ballplayer and an entertainer. This is the stance and situation to be creative and put your personal stamp on the position. I urge you to keep this in mind to break the monotony and bring some energy to your team and your game. It will also separate you from the majority of stationary backstops plaguing baseball.

Blocking/Throwing Stance

The blocking/throwing stance is the position to use when there are two strikes or men are on base. It is the most athletic squat by which to block the ball or throw out runners. From the comfort stance, shift your weight from the insteps to the balls of the feet, pointing them more toward centerfield. Then widen your stance an inch or two depending on your flexibility and comfort level. I often see catchers dropping their right foot back well behind the left foot in throwing situations. I think this is a mistake and unnecessary. At most, the toe of the right shoe should line up with the arch of the left foot. I think in most situations it's best just to keep them even. Compared with your comfort stance, your rear end will lift up an inch or two. Your back will stay straight and as perpendicular to the ground as you can get without falling back on your heels. Your weight will be centered over the balls of your feet with the head back and stacked over the shoulders, hips, and so forth.

A front and side view of the blocking/throwing stance. Relative to the comfort stance, the rear end is lifted a little, the weight is distributed more on the balls of the feet, and the throwing hand comes out from behind the body.

Keep the same mechanics with the target as you do with the comfort stance—nothing changes. The priorities are a good target and relaxed hands. Rest your glove arm on the left leg and let your fingers point upward. The only difference will be in the free hand, which comes out from behind the body to the middle of the chest area, a couple of inches behind the glove in a soft fist. This will help with your balance and facilitate a quicker exchange in a throwing situation.

The last thing I have to say about the blocking/throwing stance before we conclude is that it can be a challenge physically. You need pretty good leg strength and endurance, which you can work on and increase in the bullpen. Make sure when you are warming up pitchers or catching them in their side work that you go into the blocking/throwing stance every time the pitcher goes into the stretch. As a matter of fact, split your bullpen time equally between your comfort stance and blocking/throwing stance no matter what.

Key Stance Points

1. Here are the three distinct stances:

    - Sign stance—used when giving signals to the pitcher.

    - Comfort stance—used when no one is on base and there are fewer than two strikes; your most comfortable squatting position.

    - Throwing/blocking stance—used when there are two strikes or men are on base and the ball needs to stay in front of you.

2. The catcher is responsible for protecting the signals from the eyes of the opponent.

3. Sign stance: feet should be a shoulder width apart, parallel to each other, and pointed toward centerfield. Bend knees, keeping back fairly straight with head back. Signal hand follows the inseam of the pants, falling gently into the crotch area to obtain proper height.

4. Your routine before every pitch should be sign-target-stance: give the sign, flash the target to the pitcher, and then flow into your stance.

5. Give a good, large, relaxed target with arm resting comfortably on the left leg and the fingers pointing skyward.

6. Be creative and demonstrate some showmanship, especially in your comfort stance.

7. Your blocking/throwing stance is the most athletic of the three. Lift your rear end an inch or two higher than in the comfort stance, widen the base, place your weight over the balls of the feet, and bring the throwing hand a few inches behind the glove.

8. Stay stacked and athletic in all three of these stances.

Chapter 4

Receiving

"Simplicity is the ultimate sophistication."
—LEONARDO DA VINCI

In this section we go over the mechanics involved in catching the ball properly. Maybe more so than any section of the book, this portion centers on simplicity—cutting out all unnecessary movements to accomplish the utmost with the minimum. These are my thoughts about body positions, glove mechanics, and mental routines that help the catcher be more consistent, safe, and efficient in his receiving.

Body Positions

First, let's talk about the catcher's body and its role in receiving the ball. All movement toward a pitched ball should be initiated by the lower body. Keep your chest and head back, trying not to fall forward or lunge at the pitch. Instead, simply use your legs subtly to shift your upper body laterally into receiving position. By moving this way, you will be able to center most balls on your chest. A word of caution—notice that I said "subtly." Quick, jabby movements from the receiver are disruptive and adversely affect umpires, causing them to miss strikes. There is a fine line between being lazy (just sticking your arm out to catch the ball) and being overzealous with your lower body. All of the catcher's actions should mimic a cat: calm, subtle, and efficient.

Offset Technique

The offset technique is a method by which the catcher shifts his weight from the middle of his stance to either side in anticipation of a particular ball's movement. For

Offset technique for a pitch moving to my left and then for one sliding to my right. Notice the distribution of weight in anticipation of movement.

example, when I call a curveball from a right-hander, I distribute more weight on my left leg in anticipation of the ball sinking to the right (correct distribution of weight should be about 60 percent on the leg opposite the ball movement). It is similar to the loading up action of a hitter, only more subtle and in a squat. Foot placement depends upon which side is supporting the most weight. On a left-handed slider my weight is 60 percent on my right side—on the ball of my right foot. The other 40 percent rests on the instep of the left foot. As with all movements behind the plate, this shift should be done *quietly* and *late* (as the pitcher winds up). You don't want to throw off the pitcher's concentration by providing a moving target, and you don't want to give away the pitch to the other team.

It is important to note that the offset technique is worthless unless the catcher has the ability to anticipate the movement of the pitch. Everything starts at the moment the sign is put down, at which point you must decide how to shift. I've got to warn you that from here forward you will be hearing a lot about anticipation because I believe it to be an essential component to consistent success. I don't believe anyone to be a good enough athlete to sit behind the plate and just react to movement and consistently receive or block the ball well. The difference between an average catcher and a great catcher is often the ability to stay focused and see action before it happens.

Drop-Knee Technique

A great method to help center the ball on the chest is what I call the drop-knee technique. This approach increases lateral range and makes tough low pitches easier to receive without having to turn your glove over. At a certain point when shifting from side to side in a squat, you reach a limit and begin to fall over. Dropping a knee at this point stabilizes and balances the situation and gives you a more athletic foundation. I liked to drop my left knee because it gave my glove hand more space to work—especially on a low right-handed sinker; however, drop whichever knee is most comfortable to you.

A picture of me early in my career, demonstrating the drop-knee technique.

Let's go through a sequence involving the offset and drop-knee techniques. Upon calling a right-handed slider, I anticipate ball movement and "offset" to my left. As the pitch approaches and as my lower body sways gently to the ball, the inside of my left knee might "drop" or touch the ground as the pitch is caught. This enhances the odds of getting my chest behind the ball and, in the case of a hard right-handed sinker (in which case the left knee would drop), it clears the knee out of the way, allowing the glove hand more freedom.

There are a few things to be aware of with this technique, and they all have to do with the upper body. Make sure that the shoulders stay squared to the pitcher at all times, and do not rotate off the ball as you drop a knee. Also, be sensitive to the movement of your upper body—make sure it doesn't follow the dropping knee down. The shoulders and head must act independently of the knee; also, remember to keep the majority of your weight back and square. If you are conscious of these tendencies, the last thing I mention will not be a factor. Realize that dropping a knee can put you in a compromised position when there are runners on base. Letting your upper body follow your knee down puts you in a very un-athletic position and leaves you vulnerable to the delayed steal. Be aware and alert. By keeping your weight back and stacked, you will have no problem coming out of a drop-knee position to throw on a delay.

A couple of views of a drop-knee approach with the body staying stacked, square, and athletic. If your upper body stays back, this is an easy position to get out of.

Glove Mechanics

The catcher's glove arm extends to meet the ball in direct proportion to the distance the ball is from his chest. To put that in plain English, the farther the ball is from you, the more aggressively you attack it. This concept (attacking balls away from your body) permeates all of my teaching—be it receiving, blocking, or throwing. So, one more time: the more extreme the pitch (up, down, left, or right), the more the glove arm extends to greet the ball. Pitches that arrive within the boundaries of the catcher's body, however, should be received with more bend in the arm, no closer, however; than eight to ten inches from the chest. A fastball right down the middle should never get any closer to you than eight to ten inches. It may help you understand this concept better if you can visualize an orange traffic cone extending from the catcher's glove out toward the pitcher with the small hole centered in the glove or target. Basically, the glove should follow this triangular path, extending to catch the ball according to where it is on the cone.

As we touched upon in the previous chapter, the catcher always gives his target with his fingers pointing toward the sky. Small adjustments can be made in anticipation of a certain pitch or the type of pitcher throwing. For example, my target is going to anticipate the movement of a left-hander's slider by rotating slightly more to the left. By contrast, my target will "cheat" and rotate more to the right on a right-hander's cutter or a lefty's sinker. Once again, these movements are subtle and late, so as not to disturb the pitcher's focus on the target and not to give away the pitch to the opposition. These small tweaks in setup increase the catcher's awareness and enhance his ability to receive the ball consistently. Not only is he thinking

Examples of extension, attacking pitches on the extreme.

about the action of the pitch just being called, but he is also making a concrete physical movement (tweaking the target) to reinforce that thought. We talk more about the relationship between mental and physical phenomena and how they relate to anticipation and consistency in a later chapter.

Here are the reasons why it is beneficial to give the target with the fingers up: First, it provides a bigger surface area for the pitcher to focus on. Second, it's basically the position you want to end up in when you actually come in contact with the ball. That means from the time you give the target to the moment you receive the ball there is no wasted movement. There are only a couple of occasions when you will turn the glove over to catch the ball: when it's in the dirt and you are "picking" it or when a hard sinker or slider comes below your knees, in which case the glove makes a half-turn to greet the ball. By using the offset technique and dropping one of your knees, you should be able to work from the ground up, eliminating the need to turn the glove over.

Giving the target with the fingers pointing toward the sky.

"Chicken winging" is the result of a pitch's movement beating you. Notice the height of the elbow in relation to the glove.

Another thing about glove mechanics is to pay attention to your left elbow. It is very important that it stay below your glove at all times. This is a position of strength, helping you to stop the momentum of the ball and to alleviate thumb injuries. When you see a catcher receiving the ball with his elbow above his glove, you know he is getting beat by the pitch and his thumb is probably taking a beating. We call this "chicken winging," and it happens to the best of us. Balls sinking hard to the catcher's left are most often the culprit—so pay attention, anticipate, and head the ball off at the pass by keeping your elbow below your hand.

A different angle demonstrating a catcher getting beat and having to "chicken wing" to receive the ball.

I should mention my thoughts on "framing" the ball since so many catchers do it. For those who don't know, framing is a technique often taught whereby the receiver strives to catch the outside of a pitch and at the same time hinges his wrist and elbow so that the ball moves "naturally" toward the strike zone. My opinion is: don't do it. Besides looking goofy, what exactly is the point? Are you going to trick the umpire into thinking a marginal pitch is a strike? It is a wasted movement, it looks dumb, and umpires hate it. Simply catch the ball firmly. When the pitch and glove meet, that's where the action should stop. The catcher should have enough strength to stop the momentum of the ball so that strikes don't turn into balls. Think of a gymnast "sticking" a landing. Just "stick" the ball, hold it for a brief second, then throw it back.

Key Receiving Points

1. The most efficient way to catch a ball is the simplest and most direct. Eliminate all unnecessary actions.

2. All movement toward the ball initiates with the lower body.

3. For benefit of the umpire, make all movements subtle and smooth, not abrupt and disruptive.

4. Use the technique of offsetting or overloading weight on either leg in order to anticipate a ball's movement. Make sure to do it late and cleanly.

5. Anticipate for consistent success.

6. Dropping a knee while maintaining good athletic posture is a good method to center your body with an incoming pitch and opens the area so the glove hand can work freely.

7. The farther a pitch is from the center of your body, the more you extend to meet it. Normally, that means eight to ten inches from your chest for a ball right down the middle to a fully extended attack for pitches on the extremities.

8. A subtle rotation of the target to the left or right is a good way to anticipate pitch movement.

9. With the exception of a hard sinker or slider below your knees or a ball bounced in the dirt, there is no need to turn your glove over to receive the ball.

10. For maximum strength and safety, receive pitches with the elbow below the glove.

11. Catch the ball cleanly and firmly; do not "frame" pitches.

Chapter 5

Blocking

"Ninety percent of this game is half mental."

—YOGI BERRA

N ow let's switch gears and focus on the important technique of blocking. From the catcher's standpoint, blocking is simply keeping a pitch thrown in the dirt in front of you. I believe it to be a very much undervalued facet of the game. Being an efficient blocker stops runners from advancing, keeps double-play situations intact, keeps runners out of scoring position, and ultimately saves runs. It can be just as important to your team as an RBI. Also, it allows pitchers to go for the strikeout and stay effectively down when they can trust that the ball is not going to the backstop. As you will see, it's not hard to be consistent and effective if you've got the right mechanics and mental approach.

Anticipation

Before we get into the actual fundamentals, I would like to mention what I think is the most important component to keeping the ball consistently in front of you: the ability to anticipate. You can have poor blocking mechanics and do a great job of keeping the ball in front of you if you anticipate well. Webster's dictionary defines anticipation as the ability "to nullify, prevent, or forestall by taking countermeasures in advance." As a catcher, it is extremely important to take countermeasures and know where your pitchers miss with their pitches. Every pitcher on your staff has tendencies and misses in the same spots most of the time. If you know where those "spots" are, half the battle is over. A ball should, in effect, be blocked *before* the pitch is ever thrown. Anything less is too late and too inconsistent. Like I said before, nobody has enough athletic ability just to react and consistently block a 95 mph fastball without anticipation. You may get there once in a while, but that is not good enough to build the trust of your pitching staff and save runs when they really count.

I can hear you now, saying that you play or coach at the Pony or even high school level and that all the kids are unpredictable with their pitches. I won't deny that. Oddly enough, from an anticipation standpoint, it is probably easier to catch in the big leagues than any other level because you have a better idea of where the ball is going. If you really bear down in the bullpen and pay attention, however, you will be surprised at the patterns that develop. Even the wildest closer in Little League has tendencies, and the bullpen is where you learn them. Hard work reveals those "spots" and enables you to anticipate correctly in the game.

Let me go over my thought process in a blocking situation. Let's say I am catching Eric Gagne in the ninth inning of a game. There is one out and a runner on third; the count is 1 and 2. Thinking strikeout, I put down the signal for a hard breaking ball. I immediately visualize the pitch being thrown in the dirt in the specific area where Gagne most often misses. I know from paying attention in the bullpen that if he does miss with his curveball in that situation, it will generally finish about two feet in front and just to the right of me—about 90 percent of the time. I then make a physical movement of offsetting my weight or tweaking my glove slightly to the right in my setup. I am now thoroughly prepared for the worst-case scenario, and if he does happen to throw a strike, I simply receive the ball. As I touched upon in the section on glove mechanics, I believe that in order to be effective, anticipation must include a mental component and a physical component ("offset," glove tweak, etc.), and it must be educated by prior experience (bullpens). Do your homework in practice or before the game, and you will see your blocking effectiveness increase dramatically.

Hand, Glove, and Arm Positions

First off, we need to be clear about the role the glove plays during a blocking sequence. It is used to protect and fill the area called the "five hole" in hockey. That is the open area from your crotch to the ground, in between the thighs when you are on your knees. Never try to catch the ball in a blocking situation. The glove's only purpose is to clog that five hole—period. Repetition and practicing the proper glove mechanics frees catchers from the impulse to "pick" balls in the dirt. Receivers learn to "catch" the ball with the middle of their chests.

The throwing hand does one of two things. It can either slide behind the glove or stay somewhere outside the right hip. Although it looks a little odd and goes against traditional blocking fundamentals, having the hand outside of the body can be quite effective. It can help with balance (you end up looking kind of like a rodeo bull rider), and it has the advantage of freeing the bare hand to swat at a ball in the dirt that takes a weird hop. But, to be honest, there is really no great advantage one way or the other. Let your comfort be the judge. Personally, sometimes I would put it behind the glove, and sometimes I wouldn't.

It is important, however, to pay attention to where your arms are, particularly

Proper blocking form with throwing hand behind the glove and "rodeo style."

the biceps and elbows. Make sure that they stay outside of your body—thus providing a bigger blocking surface and decreasing the likelihood of an unpredictable ricochet. Remember that you are trying to center or "catch" the ball in the middle of the chest. It doesn't make any sense to get your arms all tangled up in the same area. Aside from all of this, it plain hurts when your arm gets hit by a ball in the dirt. To remedy this situation, it helps to keep your arms loose and tension-free during a blocking sequence. The more you anticipate contact with the ball and tense up, the more the elbows tend to come together in front of the chest. So work on increasing your blocking surface area by staying relaxed and getting your arms out of harm's way.

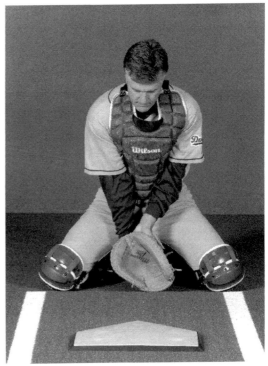

In relation to the previous images of proper blocking technique, notice the position of the arms and how in the way they are.

Body Positions and Angles

Because we try to create the largest blocking surface possible, it is obviously a good idea to avoid hunching or rounding the shoulders over the ball. Keep the head stacked on top of the shoulders with the back fairly straight. I told you this "athletic position" idea would permeate everything! The chin will move down to the chest as your eyes follow the trajectory of the ball in the dirt, protecting your throat in the process. It is at this point (actual contact with the ball) that you can let your upper body tilt forward, effectively angling the block straight down instead of off to the sides. Don't completely collapse on the ball. Just get a slight forward angle and remember that it is all for naught if you cannot get out of this position in time to bounce on a block and throw the runner out. Picture an infielder watching a grounder roll into his glove. Actually, blocking a ball is very similar to fielding a ground ball, except you are obviously on your knees and instead of using a glove to catch you are using your chest. And just like an infielder, it is extremely important

The athletic posture and slight forward angle of a properly blocked ball.

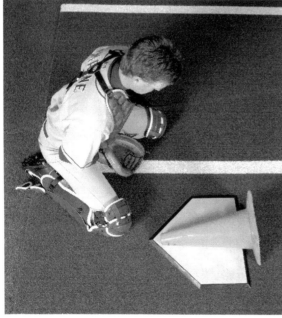

Following the direction of the cone, gaining ground, and getting an angle on a bounced ball to my left.

to stay athletic and follow the ball all the way in.

In blocking a ball, follow the same general angles used for receiving. Going back to the traffic cone image—the more the ball gets out to the extremes, the more you attack. The chalk of the first and third baselines gives you a guide to the proper angle by which to approach wild pitches to your left and right. For a ball right down the middle—but in the dirt—you simply and quickly drop to your knees. You don't gain a whole lot of ground, but you definitely do not lose any either. The farther the ball gets from your stance, the farther up the baseline you need to go to get it. Sliding laterally is ineffective because you can't get your shoulders turned, squared, and perpendicular to the trajectory of the ball. Deflections will ricochet everywhere. Make every effort to get a proper angle on all balls in the dirt, with your shoulders square to the incoming bounce. Along these lines, it's important to realize that all pitches react differently once they hit the ground. For example, fastballs follow more or less the same trajectory whereas breaking balls (because of their rotation) tend to "back up" and go the other way. Spend a little time in the bullpen familiarizing yourself with the way different pitches react with the ground, and position your body accordingly.

Efficiency and Keeping the Ball Close

Try to be efficient when you are going down to your knees for a block. Remember, a straight line to the bouncing ball is the easiest and quickest method. The common mistakes of un-weighting and going up before going down or kicking your feet back are wasted movements and take precious time. Simply get to your knees as quickly and efficiently as possible by going straight down.

The proximity of the ball to the catcher's body after he blocks it is another significant issue worth exploring. In today's game most runners are trained to take their lead off first and watch the trajectory of the ball out of the pitcher's hand. If the pitch looks like it will short-hop the catcher, they are taught to just steal. (If you aren't teaching that method or as a player you don't follow the trajectory, it's a very effective tool to add to your offensive skills.) It is imperative that the catcher develop enough body control and lower body strength to pounce on deflected balls quickly enough to be able to throw out alert runners or at least discourage them from advancing. Often times the distance (or lack thereof) the ball rolls from you will be enough of a deterrent.

In order to keep a blocked ball within three or four feet of you, it is critical that you get where you are going (with both knees down and at a proper angle) and exhale before the ball hits you. If you and the bouncing ball collide at the same time, the ball will careen too far from your body to be effective. The result will be a runner who gets to advance. It would be no different than if you didn't even try to block the ball and just ran to the backstop to pick it up after it stopped rolling. Just like in hitting, there is a timing to all of this. Get there too soon and you won't be able to adjust to changes in trajectory—too late and the ball is gonna ricochet. Even though you are gaining ground and attacking a blocked ball, make sure to create that "pillow" effect by exhaling as you and the ball meet.

Anatomy of a Proper Block

The blocking sequence accomplished successfully ends up looking something like this: Both knees are down and outside of the hips. The whole body is square, at a perpendicular angle to the trajectory of the ball. Your weight (upper body) is stacked on top of your hips—not in front or hunched over them—until you make actual contact with the ball. The glove covers the gap between the crotch and the ground with the free hand either behind it or close to the right hip. Your back is fairly straight with the arms relaxed and outside of the body. The head follows the path of the ball and comes down as the eyes watch it bounce into the dirt. You exhale, turning into a human pillow as contact is made. The ball deflects about two inches in front and, catlike, you pounce on it, throwing the bewildered runner out by ten feet. I admit as I read this back to myself that it sounds like a lot of action to compress into what amounts to the blink of an eye. I promise you, though, that with practice and proper anticipation (bullpen work), it is not that hard. You will progress quickly.

Key Blocking Points

1. Use bullpen time to figure out your pitching staff's tendencies and specific areas where they miss with certain pitches. Use this information to anticipate correctly in game situations.

2. In order to be effective, anticipation must include a mental component and a physical component, and it must be based on some prior information or experience (bullpens).

3. In blocking, the role of the glove is to cover and clog the area in between the legs. "Catch" the bounced ball with the middle of the chest; never "pick" at the ball with the glove.

4. Your throwing hand can either slide behind the glove or stay outside, near the right hip.

5. To maximize blocking surface and minimize unpredictable ricochets, keep the biceps and forearms relaxed and outside the chest and stomach area.

6. There are two components to a successful block: keeping the ball within a couple feet of you and having the ability to recover quickly and throw the ball.

7. Like a good infielder, stay athletic and see the block all the way into your chest. Remember: Balance is in the ears, and where your head goes, your body will follow.

8. Attack balls on the extremities.

9. Obtain proper angles by getting the shoulders turned, squared, and perpendicular to the trajectory of a ball in the dirt.

10. The rotation of different pitches causes them to react differently when they hit the ground.

11. A straight line is the quickest path to the ball. Get the knees to the ground as quickly and efficiently as possible by driving them straight down.

12. Relax and exhale as your body and the ball meet to create a "pillow" effect, and keep the resulting ricochet close.

Chapter 6

Throwing to Bases

Aside from a collision at the plate, throwing out potential base stealers probably ranks as the most exciting play a catcher can make. A successful putout can disrupt offensive momentum and get your pitching staff out of jams. There are many different and effective ways to throw out base stealers and, contrary to popular opinion, you do not have to have a cannon to be successful. In this section we explore the commonalities that all great throwing catchers share, including priorities, handwork and exchange, footwork and balance, timing, back picking, and pitchouts. One thing is for sure: With the speed of today's game, you have got to find a technique that will enable you to deliver the ball from your glove to the glove of the middle infielder in a maximum of two seconds.

"If one of his enemies thinks he will advance a base due to his lack of prowess with his throwing arm, watch him become the strongest arm on the team. When he has to stand out of a crouch and throw a runner out trying to steal second base, this is when he is the Gladiator of baseball. I don't know this for a fact, but I would bet you that catchers pride themselves on their percentage of runners caught stealing above their batting average."
—"DANNYE"

Priorities

First, let's discuss and rank a catcher's priorities as they relate to throwing. Exploring these ideas may help the catcher or coach decide what is most important and, in doing so, become more effective. Just as Tiger Woods might sacrifice some power and distance on his drives for accuracy in certain situations, it is important for the catcher to stay within himself and realize that it is not all about how great an arm he has. The first priority is accuracy. You must consistently throw the baseball over second base at the infielder's waist—period. If you cannot do that, everything else is irrelevant. Quickness and timing come second. I would rather have a quick release with my body underneath me and a marginal arm than a cannon with a slow release. Surprisingly, the last priority is velocity. If God blessed you with the ability to throw the ball out of the stadium, by all means don't give it back. I will say, though, that I have seen a whole bunch of arms that would make you drool but couldn't throw out the trash. Even I could steal a base! Don't get me wrong, every player should show off his arm—just make sure to do it in pre-game infield. In a game situation, be effective. More often than not, that means being in control, quick, and accurate—even if that means a loop in the throw.

I look at it this way: God either blessed you with a great arm or he didn't. You can work on and improve your arm strength, but for the most part, it is what it is. That means as far as we are concerned, velocity is out of our hands. We do, however, have the ability to improve our quickness and accuracy. Rare is the player who has all three.

The Ivan Rodriguezes of the world don't exactly grow on trees! If you possess two out of the three qualities with an average or even below average arm, you can make a lot of money in this game. For a great example of an effective thrower with an average arm (at best), watch Thurman Munson in one of those classic Yankee reruns. The point is, take control of what you can—take control of and figure out a way to be successful with what you've got.

Yankee great Thurman Munson

Handwork and Exchange

Catching is a one-handed position. Even though you bring out your free hand in a throwing situation from behind your body, it is important to remember that we do so only to help streamline the exchange. Going to the ball with two hands pulls your upper body ahead of your lower, causing you to lose your base and center of balance. Once again, use your legs to shift laterally into receiving position and then let the glove work independently of the body. Use your right hand as a kind of ballast to provide balance and to help keep your upper body back and stacked. Picture a right-handed boxer flicking jabs with his left and keeping his right back. Obviously, you don't want to be known as a "boxer" behind the plate. I use this analogy just to give you a visual of how the hands should work in relation to the body.

(top photos) Notice what happens when you go to the ball with two hands. The body stays back and balanced when the ball is received with one hand while the weight pulls forward and comes un-stacked when two hands go forward.

(bottom) A classic image of Yogi Berra and Ted Williams. Notice Yogi's two handed approach and how it pulls his body forward. Also note Williams' perfectly stacked and balanced finish.

After the ball is caught, the glove and bare hand meet about eight to ten inches in front of the chest to make the exchange. Don't jerk the ball to the right ear as is commonly taught. This is a slow, wasted movement that causes more problems than it's worth. The main issue with whipping the glove across the body to make the exchange is that it causes the left shoulder to over-close and the body to over-rotate. As I point out later, proper footwork points your shoulders and upper body in the right direction without any additional effort. The other problem with the exchange around the right ear is that it doesn't give you enough time to get a proper grip and start the arc of the arm. Your margin for error is tiny. By making the exchange eight to ten inches in front of the chest, you stay in balance and have plenty of time to grip the ball.

While we're at it, let's talk about gripping the baseball. This may sound trivial, but as the catcher develops arm strength, it's a very important component to a good throw. Simply put, always grip the ball with the fingers perpendicular to the two widest seams. This is called a four-seam grip. Just as a pitcher uses this grip when he really needs control, so does the catcher. The four seams rotating through the air provide stability and true ball flight. It's possible for a catcher to have great throwing fundamentals and footwork only to be tripped up by a ball that unpredictably sails or cuts at the end. Practice finding the four seams as quickly and consistently as possible. Flip the ball in front of you as you watch TV and find the seams—anytime is a good time to reinforce this habit and enhance your quickness.

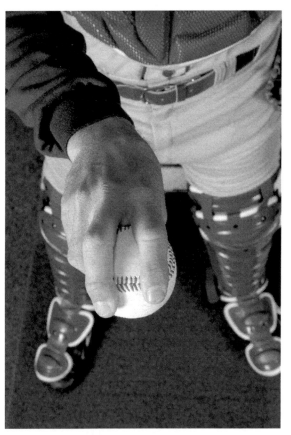

The four-seam grip

I guess it's a matter of preference, but I should mention a little bit about the glove itself and how it can affect the exchange. I was always very sensitive to pocket depth in my gloves. I liked a good pocket but did not want it so deep as to have to dig around in there to find the ball. A middle infielder doesn't use an outfield glove because making a quick exchange is a priority. The same idea applies to the receiver. Find a glove with enough pocket depth to provide comfort but not so much as to impede a quick and easy exchange.

Lower Body Movement and Footwork

I don't want to be redundant, but it is very important that your body stay under control. Make every effort to stay athletic, stacked, and powerful as you come out of the crouch to throw. It might help as we go forward to visualize a power pitcher like Nolan Ryan or Tom Seaver. We want to have that same exact balance and lower body drive as we throw.

I want to be careful when I recommend a certain type of throwing footwork because I have seen catchers succeed with many different styles. Personally, I felt most comfortable with a small jab forward with my right foot; then, I stepped with my left and threw. I used this technique on all pitches except a ball to my extreme left, in which case I wouldn't use any footwork. I would just square my shoulders and release.

The balance, power, and lower body drive of Tom Seaver.

You may be most comfortable and effective with a jump pivot or a jab with the right foot or maybe no footwork at all. Regardless of the method you choose to come out of your crouch, make absolutely sure that it directs your momentum through the pitcher toward second base. What I mean is: Do not use footwork that involves the right foot sliding under your body to replace the left foot to throw. That means your momentum is going to the left, regrouping, and then going forward. Do not use footwork in which you pop up and replace your right foot anywhere behind the point where it started. In this example your momentum is actually going backward; you then need to regroup to go forward. Finally, do not stand straight up out of the crouch (effectively losing all leg drive) to throw. Your momentum and weight go up, regroup, and then have to

go back into the legs to go forward. These are all wasted movements that disrupt balance and take too much time. Simply make sure your rise from squat to throwing position follows a gradual uphill plane and that your right foot is going forward (not to the side or backward), if it moves at all. Cut out all actions that cause your body to go in any direction but forward.

A great method for directing momentum properly is to make a small circle about six to twelve inches in front of your right foot while you are in the squat. Then draw a line out of the top of the circle pointing through the pitcher to second base. It ends up looking like an upside down lollipop. Literally draw it in the dirt. Then simply get your right foot in that circle, perpendicular to the line to second base and your left foot on the line when you throw. This cures the common problem of sliding to the left and has the added bonus of squaring your upper body and shoulders to second base without any effort at all. The only time I don't recommend this technique is on a low outside pitch to the right or if it's necessary to pick the ball out of the dirt to throw. In these two situations the options are really limited. I found the only consistently effective way to deliver the ball to second involves no footwork at all. Simply square the shoulders and go, making sure to stay loaded over the right leg and compensate for the decrease in power by adding a little more arch or "rainbow" to your throw. Ideally, the lead foot should finish no farther left than the point of home plate no matter what method is used. It is a very simple and effective technique and one that can really help with timing when you find yourself moving too fast or losing balance.

In the first image, I've swung out too far to the left relative to home plate. In a perfect world, my momentum would be directly or slightly left of home plate, driving through the pitcher toward second base, as demonstrated in the second picture.

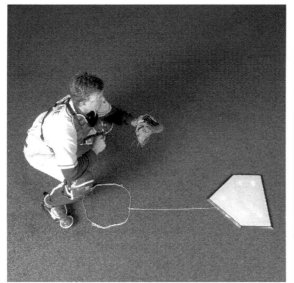 

In a throwing situation, draw the circle and line shape in the dirt directly in front of the right foot. Come up to throw, making sure the right foot is in the circle and perpendicular to the line and the left foot is on the line pointed toward second base.

Timing

Far and away, the biggest wild card in all of this is timing—in other words, figuring out when to go forward and when to wait. Just like in hitting, proper timing is everything. There is a fine line between waiting too long for the ball and going out to meet it. Generally speaking, the ball can move more quickly than you can, so wait as long as possible before starting your footwork, making sure you still have forward momentum and are not starting from a standstill. It's a matter of finding that middle ground and effectively walking the razor's edge. I will say that slower with the lower body is usually better. Most good hitters generally put a premium on staying "inside" and driving the ball the other way because they understand that most problems occur not from getting jammed but from being too far out in front. Similarly, the catcher's natural inclination is to see the runner go and immediately start leaning, drifting too far out in front. This is a killer because it causes you to unstack, pulls you away from pitches to your right, and throws off your balance. You must learn to be patient, hang back, and attack at the right time. The sequence of events from moving your feet to squaring your shoulders to making the throw must unfold in the proper order. It all happens from the ground up.

The biggest problem next to not having your momentum going in the right direction is having the left foot touch down before the exchange has allowed your throwing arm to move forward. In other words, when that lead foot hits the ground, the ball must be in the throwing hand moving forward on the upper part of the throwing arc. If the timing is not right on this, the lower body will "slip" ahead of the upper body, robbing the throw of accuracy and power. Ideally, when the arm is ready to throw, the weight should be stacked 60–70 percent over the right leg in a power position. Again, visualize a power pitcher and the drive and balance of his legs. If you attack too soon, you'll be "strung out," too late, and you will be on your heels. The techniques I offer help, but only practice, patience, and experience allow you to navigate the razor's edge of finding your personal timing.

Balanced and ready to deliver a powerful throw vs. the "strung-out" look of a mistimed sequence.

One last thing I would like to mention regarding throws to second is to pay attention to your throws back to the pitcher. Get into a habit of hitting him in the head every time. What does this have to do with pegging runners at second? Well, if you throw a ball back firmly at about head high to a pitcher standing on the rubber and

Strong throwing technique looks the same in every era. (top) Ernie Lombardi circa 1930 and (bottom) Mike Scioscia circa 1980.

he moves out of the way, guess where that ball will land. That's right, in the vicinity of second base. Your throws to second base in a steal situation have the same trajectory of a throw back to the pitcher. Since you are going to be tossing the ball back to him about 150 times a game, you might as well do it right and actually get something out of it. Aside from all of that, he will love you because he won't need to burn energy bending over to retrieve your lazy throws.

Back Picking

Back picking, or throwing behind base runners, can be a very effective weapon in a catcher's arsenal. It is important to understand that the biggest benefit to back picking is not getting outs per se, even though you will get a few. The biggest benefits are the tentativeness and fear you can plant in the minds of the opposition. Basically, it's a great tool to keep runners from getting aggressive leads and jumps. I don't know how to explain it any better than to cite Ivan Rodriguez. His biggest weapon isn't his arm. The *threat* of his arm is his biggest weapon. Trust me, you know exactly how far from the base you are when you play against that guy. The idea that he might embarrass you keeps you from getting any kind of secondary lead, much less trying to steal.

Following that thought, it makes sense to throw behind runners often—especially early in the game so you can plant a seed of fear in the mind of the opposition. If you make sure to put a priority on accuracy and do it at the right time in the game (i.e., early and when the game is not on the line), the risk is a small price to pay to keep runners anchored close to the bases. Another point to remember is never to back pick on a bad pitch. It is just too risky. Let's say you have gone to the trouble of signaling the first baseman and together you have a plan to nab an unalert runner. If the pitch

Ivan Rodriquez, a serious threat to the comfort of base runners.

comes and pulls you out of balance in the least, do yourself a favor and call off the jam. Do not pick on a bad pitch. Just remember, there isn't a big upside to rushing and risking errant throws in an effort to steal an out—it is more about the threat than actually getting outs.

A couple of final thoughts about picking: First, use a left-handed hitter to "shield" yourself when picking to first. By staying low and behind him, oftentimes the runner never sees you coming. Second, a back pick to third is best done when there are no outs (e.g., lead-off triple or runner at third and no outs) because the odds are the runner is going to score anyway. This is also best done with a left-handed hitter because you have a clear pathway. Make sure you are accurate and hit the third basemen in the chest.

Pitchouts

Besides proper footwork, the most important thing to remember about pitchouts is to be aggressive. Just because you've made the right call with a pitchout when the runner steals, it doesn't mean you've automatically got him hung out to dry. Do not take anything for granted. I don't know how many times I have botched this play because I "knew" we had the guy, and I let up or guided the throw or got lazy with my footwork. There is also the "yip" factor. Similar to the dilemma a golfer encounters when he can't make

Pudge happy because he probably just picked me off.

a smooth stroke because he's developed a phobia of missing short putts, the "yip" problem can also plague a catcher during a pitchout. It is so obvious that you should get the runner that you kind of run into a no-win situation. Like a two-foot putt, you feel you should execute this play—period. That kind of mentality can lead to paralysis and cause you to guide the ball. For me, the way out of it was not to take the play for granted and stay aggressive with all my movements. Stay focused, stay low, gain ground, and deliver a smooth, powerful throw to second base.

Just like in a regular throwing sequence to second base, your timing is crucial with a pitchout. The timing can be broken down into two parts—when actually to come out of the crouch and the synchronization of your footwork and exchange. As far as coming out of the squat goes, just make sure you stay low and come out at a gradual incline. Do not pop straight up, and be conscious not to come out of your stance too soon. Both these factors keep the power in your legs and, more significantly, do not alert the base stealer of the pitchout. If you make a move out of the squat too early, a good runner will sense you and call off the jam. Then, there is the synchronization of your footwork and exchange. Just as we talked about in the previous section, when the left foot comes down, all the handwork must be done, and the ball must be moving forward. Again, we are striving to find that fine line between moving too fast and lagging behind. Ultimately, what we want is to arrive at the point where we are in an athletic, powerful position to throw the ball when all the dust has settled.

Before we get into the actual footwork, let's talk about the angles we should follow and where to set up. Just like in the receiving, blocking, and throwing techniques presented in this book, we want to make sure we are gaining ground and have forward momentum to meet the ball. The most common mistake with pitchouts is to make the first step laterally. I look at it this way: This play should give me a distinct advantage because I get a head start on the footwork and don't need to throw from as far a distance. Going laterally definitely nullifies the second opportunity. Simply make sure your first step follows either the first or third baselines so that you are actually gaining ground and getting the advantage you've earned. The setup is simple. Depending on which side you are going to pitch out, just align the right or left edge of the plate in the middle of your crouch.

The footwork for a pitchout is slightly different depending on which side you are going. On the left side, your foot movement goes left; then you catch, move right, then left, and then throw. In other words, as the pitcher releases the ball, the catcher takes a jab step with the left foot, catches the ball, then takes a right-foot step, followed by a left-foot step, and then throws. On the right side, we have to add an extra step, and the timing is a bit different. The sequence goes: right step, left step, then catch, right step, left step, throw. The key to success when going to the right side is to make sure your initial right-foot jab step has been completed before the pitcher releases the ball. If you wait any longer, the timing gets screwed up, and you won't be able to finish all your footwork. So, again, for a pitchout to the right side, it goes: right-foot jab step (with the foot down before pitcher releases the ball), then left step, catch the ball, right step, left step, throw. I realize as I read this back to myself it sounds confusing. I promise it's not. Just go slowly and follow the directions. Stay low and make sure your first step is going in a forward direction (not laterally). Practice it to the point where all the movements in the sequence flow. In other words, your weight shouldn't stay on any one foot for more than a second. Picture a shortstop fielding a grounder and flowing through as he throws to first. Once you've mastered the simple footwork sequence, it's just a matter of getting the timing right.

Key Throwing Points

1. In order of importance, the priorities of throwing runners out are: accuracy, quickness and timing, then velocity.

2. You don't need a great arm to throw runners out consistently. You do need accuracy, quickness, and timing.

3. Show off your arm strength in pre-game warm-ups or in between innings. During the game, be effective and under control, even if that means taking some velocity off a throw.

4. In a throwing situation, even though both hands are in front of the body, go to the ball with just the glove. The right hand should stay back with the body for balance and athleticism.

5. After the ball is caught, the glove and bare hand meet about a foot in front of the chest to make the exchange.

6. Always throw with a "four-seam" grip.

7. When coming out of the crouch to throw, always rise on a gradual uphill plane, stay stacked, and drive off the back leg like a power pitcher.

8. Regardless of your chosen throwing footwork, make sure your momentum flows through the pitcher toward second base.

9. To square the body automatically and help get momentum going forward, draw a circle in the dirt directly in front of the right foot with a line coming out of the middle pointing toward second base. Simply get the right foot in the circle, perpendicular to second base, and have the left foot land on the line, toes directed toward second.

10. For maximum power and accuracy, remember that the whole throwing sequence works from the ground up and relies on proper timing. Learn to be patient when the runner goes, hanging back, staying stacked, and attacking at the right time.

11. Make a habit of throwing the ball back to the pitcher at head height.

12. Back pick early in the game, only on pitches that are easy to handle and with a priority on accuracy.

13. On a pitchout, stay aggressive, stay low, gain ground toward second base, and deliver a smooth, powerful, accurate throw.

14. On a pitchout, make the initial jab step follow the first or third baselines. Do not move laterally.

15. Pitchout footwork with a left-handed batter is: jab with left foot then catch the ball, then step right, step left, throw.

16. Pitchout footwork with a right-handed batter is: jab with right foot (before pitcher releases the ball), step left, catch the ball, then right step, left step, throw.

Chapter 7

Calling a Game and Working with Pitchers

Now we start getting into the intangibles. It's time to put on your psychologist's cap and dive into what might be the catcher's most important job. Calling a game and having a good relationship with your pitchers have more of an effect on your team than anything else you might do. It is the reason veteran catchers are at a premium and can help separate you from the masses. In this section we will go over communication with your staff, proper pitch selection, pitch counts, and pace of game, and I will rant about the current trend of coaches calling the game.

Whether it's playing the tough guy, the smart guy, or just offering words of encouragement, a good catcher knows how to get the most out each individual on his staff. Darren Dreifort and I try to figure it out.

"He doesn't take at-bats into his catching. A lot of catchers like to talk pitchers into throwing pitches that they can't hit instead of calling your game. He calls your game. He comes out there and says, 'What do you want to do?' And he sticks with it. Or he'll say, 'I don't like that. Let's think about this.' He's got experience. He studies. He's been around. I think his passion, his emotion, helps our pitching staff."

—PITCHER BILLY WAGNER ON PAUL LO DUCA

Coaches, Please Don't Call the Game

Hear me out as I get something off of my chest. It concerns the epidemic I see of coaches calling pitches from the dugout. This bothers me on so many different levels I don't even know where to start. Honestly, I think it should be outlawed and banished from the game. To begin with, how about the time it takes for the catcher to look over every single time to get a pitch selection? It drives me nuts to watch games that drag on forever as the coach satisfies his ego. I mean, what is the upside? Shouldn't the kid be learning his craft? What good are you doing as a coach if you are turning out pitchers and catchers who cannot think and make quality decisions for themselves? It's like graduating from school and not knowing how to read. Trust me—coaches don't call pitches in pro ball. And the way things are going, amateur baseball is unleashing heaps of brain-dead players into the professional ranks. Yes, kids are going to make mistakes; yes, they are going to make stupid decisions. But that is how they learn. As pitching great Christy Mathewson wisely stated, "You can learn little from victory. You can learn everything from defeat." Calling a game is a huge part of a catcher's and pitcher's development. Having a coach call the games stunts growth.

The bottom line, anyway, is: The best pitch a kid can throw is the one he can unleash with conviction, even if it's not the perfect choice. There is no way he can do that if the pitch is coming from the dugout. Talk about handcuffs. How about the little subtleties and changes only the catcher can notice in a hitter's stance? The coach can't possibly see that from his perch. How can a receiver anticipate and plan ahead when he is just robotically putting down signals? None of it makes any sense, and it drives me crazy. You may see pro catchers glancing into the dugout to get signs and think that if it's good for them, it's good for you. Let me tell you that except for rare instances, these glances have nothing to do with pitch selection. They almost always deal with controlling the running game—when to pitch out, throw over, slide step, and so forth. If you pay close attention, you will notice that pro catchers rarely look over when no one is on base. To be honest, if I were the manager, I would let the battery control the running game, too. But that is a whole different subject. Don't get me started!

A compromise that benefits everyone is to devise a simple signal to be able to let the catcher know when you absolutely must have a certain pitch. Also, let the catcher have a signal to alert someone in the dugout that he needs help. This is a tool that I used all the way to the final years of my career. It provides a great safety net (especially when the catchers are just learning) because sometimes in the heat of the action you get confused and need a different perspective.

I was very fortunate to play for coaches and managers who never put the handcuffs on me. They would make corrections when I was wrong and suggestions when appropriate; however, they never stunted my growth by taking away the reins. As a result, the ability to call a good game and the subsequent trust that developed with my staff turned out to be my strong points. They kept me in baseball a long time and made the house payments. I am very grateful to my coaches for trusting me and seeing me through the learning curve. So, please, coaches, take your hands off the steering wheel and let go of some of the control. Teach your players well, and then unleash them on the game to do what they will. A smarter, better developed athlete will emerge, the pace of the game will improve, and, trust me, the decisions won't be half bad—maybe even better than yours.

Communicating with Pitchers

It is very important for you and your staff to be on the same page. Take the time to know your pitcher's likes and dislikes and find out where he feels his limits are. Pay attention and use the bullpen to gain insight. Communicate and ask questions. Ask him to list his pitches in order of his confidence level. Ask questions like: Do you like to throw the fastball up when ahead in the count? Do you like to bounce your breaking ball in the dirt? If we are in a strikeout situation, what is your best "out" pitch? As a catcher, you want to get to the point where you and the pitcher are of the same mind. Your pitch choices are the same as his. As he stands on the rubber and decides on the next pitch, you want your signal to more or less take the words right out of his mouth. Nothing is better than when a pitcher and catcher are on the same wavelength and together slice through the opposing lineup.

Taking the time to communicate and learning how to call a good game helps you earn the trust of your staff. You want to be known as a catcher who is not a box of rocks. Having the ability to put down the right signs takes a huge load off the pitcher's shoulders by letting him focus on execution rather than choices. Yogi Berra summed it up nicely when he wisely stated, "Think! How the hell are you gonna think and hit [or pitch] at the same time?" Helping shoulder the mental load of pitch calling can help your staff concentrate on what's important: throwing strikes. The only downside to all of this is that you never get a day off because your pitchers only feel comfortable when you are behind the plate.

Eric Gagne and I celebrate after a win.

Pitch Selection and Pitch Counts

I don't have an enormous amount of information regarding proper pitch selection because what might be right for one situation won't fit another situation. A huge list of variables must be filtered through the mind of the catcher, and they are constantly in flux. Some of the components affecting the decision-making process are the strengths of the particular pitcher, the weaknesses of the hitter, the game situation, and the umpire, to name just a few. Like I said, the list goes on and on and is rarely the same twice. Even though there is nothing written in stone, I do have a few suggestions, opinions, and guidelines that might help.

The catcher's primary focus should be to help the pitcher get outs as quickly and efficiently as possible. Keep your pitcher focused, and don't let him get caught up in the thrill of making hitters look bad or the trap of trying to make a perfect pitch. Realize that the idea is not so much to "trick" hitters but rather to pound the strike zone in good locations, resulting in quick outs. Keep the pitch count down. Make the opposition swing the bat often and early by keeping your pitcher around the strike zone. I'll take a first pitch ground out over a strikeout any day of the week. Both scenarios result in an out; however, the ground out requires only one pitch whereas the strikeout takes at least three. Over the course of a game, those numbers can really add up. Keep the pitcher focused on being efficient rather than wasting energy on something else.

Along those same lines, it's important for the catcher, coach, and pitcher to realize that there's rarely a pitch you just can't throw to someone. Usually, even a "bad" pitch selection thrown in the right spot will work. From years of experience seeing thousands of outs, I can tell you that more often than not success or failure depends on the location of the pitch. I will say that again: location, location, location. It's like real estate. That being said, don't fall into the trap of setting up on the corners too much or letting the pitcher get too "fine." If he is obsessed with throwing the ball in the perfect location (i.e., down and right on the corner), then unless his name is Greg Maddux, he is not going to be throwing a lot of strikes. You don't want to put the hitter in the driver's seat by getting yourself in counts where you have to pipe a fastball. Again, make hitters swing the bat and get quick outs by pounding the strike zone early with quality pitches.

The last thing to mention on the subject of what pitch to call is always to go with your pitcher's strength. For example, if confusion arises because a certain hitter is known as a great change-up hitter but that is also your pitcher's best pitch, go with the change-up. Again, if that is the pitcher's best chance of throwing a strike in a good location and he can do it with conviction, then that is the best choice no matter what the scouting report says. Always call the game according to your pitcher's strength instead of the hitter's weakness.

Pace of Game

As a catcher, you control the pace of the game. You're kind of like a point guard in basketball. You can push the ball up the court and play the fast break game or you can slow it down and stall. The speed pedal is under your foot, and by toying with it you can control momentum shifts. I'm not going to lie—as a general rule, I have a heavy bias for pushing the action. I love quick play and recommend it for a number of reasons. That being said, when the offense was rolling and crushing my pitcher, I definitely tried to break the opposing team's momentum by slowing down the action. Outside of that situation, though, I tried to put the signs down quickly and confidently and felt that doing so positively impacted my team. How so? Well, for one thing, I liked to get my pitcher in the groove of getting the ball, getting on the rubber, and letting it go. Like I've said before, the less time a pitcher has to think, the better. Pushing the action also keeps your defense on its toes. I know from playing middle infield that there is nothing worse than a pitcher who takes a minute in between every pitch. How about this reason—fans love quick games. But probably the biggest and best reason for speeding up play is that you take the opposition out of its comfort zone. In general, ballplayers know how to play the game at one speed—slow. Most have no idea how to compete at a quick pace. Pushing the issue by getting the ball back to the pitcher right away and quickly putting down the signal makes good sense if for no other reason than it makes the opposition uncomfortable.

Key Game Calling and Communication Points

1. Calling a game and having a good relationship with the pitching staff are the most important jobs of a catcher.

2. Coaches, teach your battery the game plan, and then turn them loose to call their own games.

3. Earn the trust of your pitchers and ease their workload by asking questions, taking time to learn their preferences for certain pitches, understanding their limits, and using this information to make informed decisions.

4. Help the pitcher get outs quickly and efficiently. Keep the pitch count down by pounding the zone in good locations, resulting in quick outs.

5. Location is more important than the type of pitch.

6. When in doubt about which pitch to select, always go with the pitcher's strength instead of the hitter's weakness.

7. The catcher controls the pace of the game. Except in situations where you are trying to slow the momentum of the opposition, get the ball back to the pitcher and put the signs down quickly and confidently.

Chapter 8

Pop Flies

*"He hit a pop-up against us one day that went so high,
it was higher than the sun. It was up there so high, all
nine guys on our team called for it."*
—RICH DONNELLY ON MARK MCGWIRE

Pop flies can be either a disaster or a pretty basic play for a catcher. In this brief section, we go over what you can expect from a ball in the air and the proper techniques to execute this relatively simple play.

First off, let's cover the trajectory of a pop fly as it relates to the catcher. If a batter swings at a pitch, the only way it will pop straight up is if the bat just clips the bottom half of the ball. It is important to note that this type of contact creates a tremendous amount of backspin, causing the ball to take a banana-shaped trajectory as it descends from its apex (from the stands toward the infield). This means the ball will not be dropping straight down out of the sky; it will curve. From its apex, the pop-up will travel in a crescent shape from the stands to you. This means that if the catcher remains facing the infield when he attempts to make this play, he is going to have serious problems. Essentially, he will need to make a Willie Mays over-the-shoulder type of catch. It is very important that the receiver immediately turn his back to the infield and keep some space between himself and the ball as it tumbles from the sky. As it descends, you do not want to feel like you're centered under the ball, because if you do, you will need to do some quick back stepping to follow it. Keep the ball in front of you in anticipation of its path. It's kind of like receiving a curveball, except you look straight up.

*The banana-shaped path
a foul ball takes as it falls
from the sky.*

Before turning his back to the infield, the catcher needs to take the mask off and find the ball. Once the ball is located, throw the mask in the opposite direction of where you are going. You don't want to get your feet tangled up with it as you try to track the pop fly.

Like a good outfielder, you should go to the ball on the balls of your feet and try not to drift. Pursuing pop-ups flatfooted jars your vision, and the ball seems to bounce in the air because your eyes are bouncing. By almost tiptoeing to the ball, you keep your eyes stable, and the ball doesn't appear to pinball around. What do I mean by "try not to drift"? Try to get to the general area where the ball will land as soon as possible. Like an outfielder who finds the wall and then goes to the ball, make sure to find any obstacle, and then back away from it instead of drifting into it. For example, if I see a pop fly is going toward the stands or dugout, I bust my butt immediately to that area, so I know exactly where I am, and then I back off or dive in to make the play. I do not allow the trajectory of the ball to lead me around, because by looking straight up at the ball, I'm essentially blind to any obstacles that might be in my path. The last thing to mention is to be sensitive to changes in the direction of the wind and sun as the game rolls on. Both change often and can have a huge impact on both your ability to see and the downward flight of the ball.

Johnny Bench, Mickey Cochrane, and I go for pop flies.

Key Pop-up Points

1. Pop-ups descend in a crescent shape, curving from the stands to the field.

2. To catch a foul ball properly, turn your back to the infield and throw the mask in the opposite direction of the play.

3. Get to the point where you think the pop fly will end up as quickly as possible by running on the balls of the feet.

Chapter 9

Plays at the Plate

"Ninety feet between home plate and first base may be the closest man has ever come to perfection."

—RED SMITH

In addition to being the most dangerous play for a catcher, a play at the plate is one of the most exciting moments in all of baseball. Anticipation and energy build as the paths of an incoming throw and runner align, eventually coming to a crescendo in a collision or slide play at the plate. In the midst of such chaos, a catcher must keep his wits about him, keep his vision of the whole field, and employ proper tagging and blocking techniques to ensure safety and effectiveness.

"Then, when there is a close play at his prized piece of real estate, his sacred ground, home plate, watch as he gives up life and limb to block any access. Some of the most memorable moments in baseball have come in the form of collisions worthy of the WWF."

—"DANNYE"

Gabby Hartnett hanging in there for a play at the plate.

Maximize Peripheral Vision

A catcher must have and keep full vision of the unfolding play in order to make good decisions and anticipate contact at home plate. In order to maximize peripheral vision, stay a good four or five feet behind the dish for as long as possible and move into the play as it develops. In other words, do not jump up to the front of the plate as soon as the ball is hit, because the view from that angle won't allow you to see all the unfolding action. Staying back enables you to track the progress of a runner rounding third (especially on a ball down the right field line) and enhances your ability to make the correct decision regarding a possible play at home or a cut to one of the other bases. Having full vision of the play also eliminates unnecessary contact with the runner because you will know if you need to block the plate or if you have enough time to tag and get your body out of the way. I don't mind contact at the plate; as a matter of fact, I kind of like it. I don't, however, like the disabled list, and I'm very aware that a runner hitting you at full speed is probably the quickest way to end up on it. With that in mind, keep it safe and simple and block the plate when necessary, but tag and avoid the contact when possible.

Sometimes even Hall of Famers got it wrong. Mickey Cochrane had to dive back to make a tag.

Know Where You Are

The catcher must always know where he is in relation to home plate. With all the energy flying around as the play develops, it is really easy to lose track of where you are and wander off from your post. I don't know how many times I've seen a catcher screw up a great throw from an outfielder because he drifted way up in front of home plate, then needed to dive all the way back to make a tag. To remedy this situation, we have specific spots to position the left foot as you move into the play. For a ball down the left field line, the left foot goes on the left front corner of the plate. For a ball toward center, it goes on the front middle. For a ball down the right field line, the left foot goes on the right front corner. These spots serve as a kind of "anchor" and keep you from creeping out of position. In order to prevent knee injury, try to point your toes down the third baseline and keep your weight over your right leg in all three of these spots. This ensures that if the runner slides into you early, he will hit your shins instead of the sides of the knee. The last thing to note is to keep your shoulders squared to the incoming throw.

Tagging and Blocking the Plate

It's funny; after being around the game for thirty-plus years—catching over a thousand games in the big leagues—I pretty much thought I had the tag and block at the plate thing figured out. Then, recently, I gave a lesson to a minor leaguer who plays in the Los Angeles Angels organization. I should say he gave me a lesson, because I learned a much better way of executing the play. It just goes to show you that if you have an open mind, this game never stops teaching you. This technique originated from manager and ex-big leaguer Mike Scioscia. In baseball circles, he's widely regarded as the all-time blocker of home plate, and I am privileged to share what I know of this technique with you.

Proper placement of the feet and body in anticipation of a play at home plate for a ball coming from left field, centerfield, and right field, respectively.

To explain it, let me set up a situation. Let's say there is a runner on second base late in the game and the batter singles to centerfield. Now the action unfolds. By staying back and using peripheral vision, you know there is going to be a play at the plate and that there won't be time to tag and get out of the way. It's going to be a bang-bang play. Your left foot is correctly positioned in its anchor spot, and your weight is mostly over your right leg. As you receive the incoming throw, push off with your right leg while driving both knees to the ground. Use your momentum to slide on your shin guards, with your rear end on your feet toward the third base dugout. You should end up in front of (i.e., blocking) home plate with your knees parallel to each other but

Rick Ferrell flowing into good plate-blocking form.

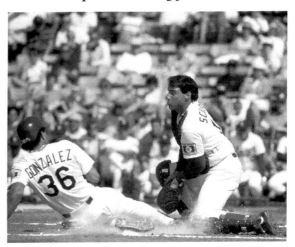

The master, Mike Scioscia, demonstrating his signature blocking technique.

perpendicular to the third baseline. Your shoulders should be square to the runner, and you should be sitting on your calves. The insides of both legs should touch one another, and the right toes should be over the left as you apply the tag and brace yourself for contact.

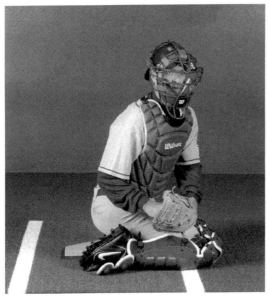

Properly completed form for blocking the plate.

Okay, let's discuss what all of this accomplishes, and why it is better than just tagging the guy out. This technique is great because it gives you some momentum into the play, takes away home plate from the runner, and puts your body in a surprisingly safe position. By sliding into the play on your knees, you gain some speed and are not just a sitting duck. It also makes you tag aggressively. If the runner tries to slide, he will never make it to home plate, and you will be safe because he will be crashing into the side of your right shin guard. Having both knees together perpendicular to the incoming runner with your left toes under the right is a great position to be in if he tries to run you over. You cannot get any lower, and all you do is roll backward to absorb the contact. No body parts resist his forward momentum, and, as a result, you suffer no blown-out knees or ankles. Just remember that even though your knees and legs are perpendicular to the runner, your shoulders are turned and square to him.

There are a couple of final things to note regarding a play at the plate. First, keep your mask on. Whoever said you cannot see as well with the mask on must be out of his mind. If you can see a fastball coming at you, why shouldn't you see a throw from the outfield? You need all the protection you can get. Keep the mask on. Second, try to make all tags with two hands. There will be times when you will only have time to swipe a tag with the glove; however, contact with the runner makes the ball pop out, so increase your odds of success by using two hands whenever possible.

Pat Borders living dangerously, without a mask.

Key Play at the Plate Points

1. Staying four or five feet behind the plate and moving into the play as it develops increases peripheral vision, enhances the ability to make good decisions, and eliminates unnecessary collisions.

2. Use the left foot anchor spots to keep from drifting out of position.

3. Make sure the left foot and knee are pointed up the third baseline and that your weight is mostly over the right leg for safety in the event of early contact at the plate.

4. Use the "Mike Scioscia technique" for blocking home plate safely and tagging aggressively with momentum.

5. In a play at the plate, keep the mask on and use two hands to make the tag.

Chapter 10

Drills

"Do it right or don't do it at all."
—MIKE MAYNE

N ow that you have my thoughts on the catching position, I would like to share some of my favorite drills to help you enhance and practice the techniques we have covered. You may have heard this before, but it's worth repeating: Practice does not make perfect; practice makes permanent. In other words, if you have poor technique when you practice, that is what you will take out to the game. If you practice doing things the right way, you'll do them right during an actual game. Like my dad said, "If you are going to do it, you might as well do it right." I urge you to execute these drills mindfully. Pay attention to your posture and take your time to get things right. It is not so much the quantity of practice; it's the quality.

Bullpens

Bullpens are far and away the most effective places for drills a catcher has. Again, I urge you to pay attention and get something out of this time. Trust me; I know the pain and monotony of having to catch half the staff in their side work. Bullpens can either be a tiresome chore or a great opportunity to work on things. Remember, practice makes permanent. If you are lazily passing the time in the bullpen with poor mechanics, then that is probably what you will take out into the game. So, be purposeful and challenge yourself to stay focused. You're going to have to do it anyway, so you might as well get something out of it.

Here are some suggestions for the bullpen. Try to re-create game situations in your head. Go to your blocking stance at least half the time or when the pitcher is practicing his stretch. Block the balls that bounce. Pay attention and learn each pitcher's tendencies (where he misses, etc.), as well as the capabilities of your pitching staff. Make sure your pitchers finish their bullpen practice with a couple of pitchouts to each side; you get to work on your timing and footwork, and they get to practice their location. Work on your throwing footwork. Try different styles of stances. If you happen to find yourself dragging and your legs feel like lead, just go to a knee and focus on your receiving skills. The list of things you can practice in the bullpen is endless. Just use your imagination, stay engaged, and pick something to work on.

Receiving Drill

The best drill to promote soft hands and enhance concentration is what I call the "soft-hand drill." Have someone stand about thirty feet away and throw a tennis ball firmly to you. Do not use a glove. Work on receiving the ball with your elbow below your hand and concentrate on seeing the ball all the way in. This exercise exposes any shortcomings you might have, because catching the bouncy tennis ball with a bare hand demands perfection. Receiving a baseball with a glove will be easy if you can excel at this drill.

Blocking Drills

I recommend the "five-ball drill" as a warm-up or as an exercise to practice perfecting technique. With the catcher in his stance behind home plate, place one baseball on the front center of the plate and one on each of the front corners. These represent fastballs to be blocked down the middle and to the corners. To complete the line, add a tennis ball on each end about a foot and a half farther outside to represent bounced breaking balls. For the first half of this exercise, have the catcher set up down the middle and block the fastballs on the corners and down the middle, concentrating on form and control more than anything. Then move on to the breaking balls by using the offset stance (the catcher should be in this stance in anticipation of movement) and proper form. Keep in mind that curveballs react differently from fastballs when they ricochet off the dirt, and make sure to adjust your angles appropriately. Do this portion of the drill at about half speed, keeping your focus on technique.

In the second half of the drill, a coach kneels down about six or seven feet in front of the line of balls and faces the catcher. The coach raises his hand and quickly points to one of the balls, and the receiver reacts by blocking appropriately and bouncing up as if to complete the play. This part of the drill is about speed and body control. As such, it is important that the coach point to the ball assertively and quickly. You will find that the catcher will mimic the speed of the coach's point—if it's slow, he will move slowly; if it's fast, he will move quickly.

A couple of other thoughts about these exercises: With all blocking drills except the "quick-ball drill" (described below), use only one ball and make sure to see the play to its completion. Blocking the ball is one thing; having the ability to pounce on it and throw out a runner is another. Keeping the ball in front is only half of the equation. Finish the play by quickly gathering yourself and tossing the ball back at chest height. The second thing to remember is to make sure the person throwing the balls in the dirt throws them fairly hard. This is not to make the catcher tough; it is just to try to mimic a true bounce. If the ball is thrown softly, it will ricochet in unrealistic directions.

The five-ball technique, a great way to warm up and perfect blocking mechanics.

A really fun drill to promote quick feet, body control, and strength is what I call the "quick-ball drill." In this one, the coach stands about thirty feet away with as many balls as he can hold. He then unloads—skipping them as quickly as possible at the catcher. The receiver must block the ball, then return to his stance to block the next ball, and so on as rapidly as possible. It is a frantic drill from both ends. As a coach, don't wait for the catcher to get up and back into his stance—simply unload the balls in front as quickly as possible. As a catcher, you must keep your upper body stacked and develop enough strength and quickness to ensure your knees touch the ground and come up immediately without using you hands for help.

This next drill is the litmus test for your blocking skills. If you can do this well, you can block. I call it the "ball-in-the-dirt or strike" drill. The coach stands halfway between home plate and the pitcher's mound and throws either a strike or a ball in the dirt. What makes it hard is the coach doesn't tell the catcher which one is coming. Obviously, if the ball is in the dirt, the catcher blocks it, and if it is a strike, he tries to receive it without falling to his knees. This drill develops great reflexes and early pitch recognition because the coach is throwing the ball hard from about half the normal distance. The catcher must react twice as fast as his game speed without the aid of anticipation. If you can do this well, you will enjoy the confidence of knowing you can relax and wait—reacting in the game will seem like a piece of cake.

Throwing Drills

The best throwing drill I can offer any ballplayer is long-toss. For most of my career, I had the misconception that playing long catch would tire my arm out and, as a result, only participated once or twice a week. It wasn't until my last few years that I played long-toss every day, and what a difference it made. To my surprise, I did not become fatigued and my arm strength went through the roof. Warm up slowly and increase the distance between your partner all the way to the point where your best arced throw one-hops him. Stay at that distance for a dozen or so throws, paying special attention to your posture and consciously driving with your legs. Let your lower body do most of the work. If you are on the receiving end, a great way to maximize this time is to pretend that the one-hopped throw is coming from the outfield and practice your tag mechanics—a perfect example of practice with a purpose.

Finish up your long-toss session by throwing balls the distance between second base and home plate. On a regular-sized field, that means about forty-two paces from the foul line out toward centerfield. In my junior college days, my father had a piece of tape on the fence marking the correct length. Simply squat down in your throwing stance and put the ball in your glove. Pretend you have just caught a pitch and the runner is going. Use the appropriate footwork and exchange mechanics as you throw the ball back to your partner chest high.

The next couple of drills were favorites of mine for staying stacked and powerful during a throw and for fine-tuning my timing. For the first part, have a coach or a teammate stand where a hitter would stand. Have him hold a bat straight out over the plate about chest high. Simply catch the ball and go through your throwing footwork, making sure to go under the bat as you come out of the crouch. This keeps you from popping straight up and losing your legs. You are forced to come out like a jet taking off. Another way of attacking the issue and improving your timing in the process is to have a coach squat down right behind the receiver and hold onto the catcher's back belt loop. Have the coach hold onto the loop, keeping the catcher back and down until the proper moment of attack. Most receivers see a runner going and, like a hitter fooled by a change-up, drift forward with their upper body. This leads to a whole slew of problems. Having a coach hold you back familiarizes you with proper timing and the feeling of throwing from a powerful base.

Key Drill Points

1. Do the drills right or not at all. Remember, it's more about quality than quantity.

2. Bullpens are a catcher's most effective place for drills.

3. The "ball-in-the-dirt or strike" drill is the best way to increase blocking ability, quickness, and pitch recognition.

4. The best way to increase arm strength is to play long-toss.

Chapter 11

The Qualities of a Big Leaguer

"You gotta be a man to play baseball for a living, but you gotta have a lot of little boy in you."

—ROY CAMPANELLA

So how do regular old people reach the highest levels of their chosen fields? How does a kid from the Dominican Republic or Orange County, California, get to the major leagues? In this section I explore these questions. I also share a little more of my story and compare it with the stories of many of my teammates and opponents so you can get an idea of the similarities. Maybe it will provide you with a blueprint or at least answer some of your questions about what it takes to make it to the top. Maybe it will give you some motivation.

Time Spent

This may seem obvious, but it's worth stating: One trait common to all the players at the top is that they've played a ton of baseball, more baseball in fact than about 99.9 percent of the population. When all the other kids were playing video games or chasing girls, these guys were playing ball. Case in point: As of this writing, do you know where the best baseball players come from? The Latin American countries: Puerto Rico, Dominican Republic, Venezuela, and Mexico, to name just a few. Why is that? Do those countries just breed better athletes? Something in the water? Nope. The answer is plain as day. If you were to go to the Dominican Republic and walk through any town, you would see. The youth in these countries play a heck of a lot more baseball than the majority of kids in America. And that is why they are better. They don't have better gear. They aren't better athletes. They don't have better leagues.

Most of the time, they don't even have fields. They also don't have Play Stations and a lot of the distractions that kids here have.

Don't get me wrong: I am not advocating year-round organized baseball. Matter of fact, I don't like that idea much at all. There is a thing called burnout, and with the pressures of winning and losing, it can happen at a pretty early age. Play all the sports, have fun, be a well-rounded athlete, be a kid. I *am* recommending you play a lot of baseball and be around the game as much as you can. Pick up games in the park, over the line, three flies up. How about a tee in the garage and a net for some swings after homework? How about catch against the garage? Figure out ways to have a good time with a bat, ball, and glove. Trust me—they are doing it in places like Venezuela, and oftentimes they're using rocks (little tiny ones), sticks, and milk cartons for gloves. And these kids are going to be the next superstars.

A Lucky Kid

Personally, I lucked into it. My dad was a baseball coach, and since we had only one car, I had to go to the field every day after school till practice was over to go home—whether I liked it or not. As a result, I played and watched a lot of baseball. (I also spent more time eating the crap underneath grandstands than any kid ever, but that is another story.) I was also fortunate to be around a number of my dad's players who went on to be successful big leaguers. In my young mind, I figured that if they could do it, I sure as heck could. They were just normal guys like anyone else. The big leagues sure didn't seem like some mystical, far-off, unobtainable place. I knew some of the guys playing there, and my father yelled at many of them more than he yelled at me. If they could do it, so could I.

I simply made my mind up. I was just going to keep playing baseball. There was no plan B. I had a very clear picture of myself playing with the best players in the world. And for no good reason, I felt like that was where I belonged. Believe me, I was a below average player at just about every level I ever played, until I got to college. As is most often the case at the younger levels, the best players are the more developed, stronger ones. That was not me. I was a late bloomer. So it certainly wasn't great accomplishments that led me to believe I was a big leaguer. I just made it up in my head. Simple as that.

You Gotta Believe

The point I am trying to make with all of this is you need to believe in yourself. Nobody, and I mean nobody, can do that for you except you. I can give you the greatest techniques and drills in the world. It doesn't mean squat unless you believe in yourself. I can't provide that for you. You have heard it many times before: Baseball is a game of failure. Get a hit three out of every ten times, and you are a star. That could mean striking out seven times out of ten! Do you have enough confidence in yourself to think you are great after you have struck out seven consecutive times? How does o for 40 sound? Can you still believe when you've made forty outs in a row? Let me tell you, that is what it takes. To a man, every great player has been through these tribulations and popped out the other side with their faith in themselves intact. Are they ignorant? Arrogant? Smart? To be honest, I don't know—maybe a combination of all these. I do know they are tough. Reaching the highest levels and having that kind of faith requires serious mental toughness. The good news is that it can be learned and cultivated. The other good news is that it can be applied and enhance all parts of your life. It's a personal matter, and it's up to you to navigate the labyrinth of your mind to find your belief. I can give you one clue: Don't base your self-worth on your results (especially when you are young and success depends on who is the strongest). Results will come and go, some good and most bad, regardless of your athletic prowess. Seeking reinforcement from something so ephemeral puts you in the front seat of the biggest roller coaster you have ever been on. I've been on it. And I will tell you from experience that it's exhausting, no fun, and will burn you out in a big hurry.

Regardless of your outcomes, get a clear picture of yourself being great, and don't let anyone or anything take that away from you. You *do not* need to be a great athlete to play in the big leagues. You *do* need to feel like you belong there. There are no exceptions. Every great player saw himself being great in his mind's eye before he became great. And every great player has to have the mental strength and stubbornness to hang onto that picture no matter what the results or what people say.

So part of it was being born into a lucky situation. I was around a lot of great players at a young age, had access to all the equipment you could ever imagine, had a father who knew the game inside and out. The bottom line, though, is that I took advantage and played a lot of ball, and I believed in my bones that I could compete and do well at any level. Even when I wasn't at the field with all the gear, I was in the park playing all sorts of pick-up games, having fun, and honing my skills in the process. Trust me when I tell you that every player in the big leagues has a similar story, without exception. They may not have had all the opportunity, parenting, and gear, but somehow they managed to find a way to play more ball than 99.9 percent of the people in the world. And as they were wearing out the wall of the garage or playing stickball in the alley, they all stumbled upon the golden key that unlocked a strong belief in themselves. That, mixed in with some God-given talent and some luck, is why they are making the big bucks and living the dream. You can do it, too.

Chapter 12

Conclusion

"The game begins the moment you forget you are playing."

—ANONYMOUS

So that's about it. You now have the basics of what I have learned from thirty-plus years of baseball experience. Like I said earlier, by no means is this the end. Catching and baseball in general will never be "mastered." It is a work in progress, and there's always room for improvement. It's up to you to take the torch and devise more efficient, simpler ways to approach the craft. Maybe you will be the player or coach who takes these teachings and transcends them, pushing the envelope of catching to new frontiers. Watch good athletes and pay attention to good receivers. As Yogi Berra said, "You can observe a lot just by watching." Apply the basics of a good athletic foundation, and make these techniques fit your unique physiology and personal style.

I would also like to offer some wisdom from the martial arts master Bruce Lee regarding reaching your potential and the pitfalls of this or any method:

Though they play an important role in the early stage, the techniques should not be too mechanical, complex, or restrictive. If we cling blindly to them, we shall eventually become bound by their limitations. Remember, you are expressing the techniques and not doing the techniques. If somebody attacks you, your response is not Technique No. 1, Stance No. 2, Section 4, Paragraph 5. Instead, you simply move in like sound and echo, without any deliberation. It is as though when I call you, you answer me, or when I throw you something, you catch it. It's as simple as that—no fuss, no mess.

Learn these techniques then forget them and play

Remember, above all, that baseball is a game and is best played as such. Don't drag something you did offensively into your defense or vice versa. There is a whole lot of failure that comes with this game. If you learn how to let go and focus on what is happening right now, you will lift yourself above most and enjoy yourself infinitely more. The best players I ever played with or against approached the game like a little kid—in the moment.

As a catcher, your defense is what helps your team the most, so focus on that. Bring some of your own personal style and flair to the position. Be aware of your surroundings, and alert others to game situations. Be creative, be entertaining, play hard, take control of the game, and—most important—have fun.

Hall of Fame catcher Mickey Cochrane.

Steve Yeager demonstrating a creative comfort stance with Dave Parker hitting.

Bob Boone using the drop-knee approach to receive a high pitch. Notice how his upper body stays back and perpendicular to the ground.

Good examples of the "1970s Johnny Bench" style of catching. These are also good examples of how to get your fingers dislocated.

Good athletic posture looks the same in all aspects of the game. Below, the legendary Hank Aaron demonstrates perfect balance, staying stacked and ready to deliver a powerful swing.

Base stealers like Rickey Henderson stretch the limits of a catcher's skills.

Sometimes in the heat of battle we lose our cool. Here I am arguing with umpire Mike Reilly over a play at the plate. Sorry, Mike, I probably overreacted.

For a catcher, collisions at the plate come with the territory. Sometimes you give and sometimes you take. Here I am delivering a couple of blows and then receiving one.

Appendix

Additional Quotations

"Baseball is like church—many attend, but few understand."
— WES WESTRUM

"Baseball gives you every chance to be great. Then it puts every pressure on you to prove that you haven't got what it takes. It never takes away that chance, and it never eases up on the pressure."
— JOE GARAGIOLA

"If you're not having fun in baseball, you miss the point of everything."
— CHRIS CHAMBLISS

"We're ballplayers. We fail most of the time."
— DAVE HENDERSON

"Sometimes a hitter gets a hit, sometimes I strike them out, but in neither case does anyone die."
— ORLANDO "EL DUQUE" HERNANDEZ

"When you're through learning, you're through."
— VERNON LAW

"I think there are only three things America will be known for two thousand years from now when they study this civilization: the Constitution, jazz music, and baseball."
— GERALD EARLY

"The guy with the biggest stomach will be the first to take off his shirt at a baseball game."
— GLEN DICKEY

"Out of the eighty major league baseball players who have committed suicide, thirteen percent were catchers. This is second only to pitchers, who make up a whopping forty-five percent. This means that almost two-thirds of the suicides in professional baseball have come from the battery."

—ANONYMOUS

"Bob Gibson's the luckiest pitcher I've ever seen.... He always picks the night to pitch when the other team doesn't score any runs."

—TIM MCCARVER

"All pitchers are liars or crybabies."

—YOGI BERRA

"In baseball, you don't know nothing."

—YOGI BERRA

"I never blame myself when I'm not hitting. I just blame the bat, and if it keeps up, I change bats. After all, if I know it isn't my fault that I'm not hitting, how can I get mad at myself?"

—YOGI BERRA

"I think Little League is wonderful. It keeps the kids out of the house."

—YOGI BERRA

"Little League is a very good thing because it keeps the parents off the streets."

—YOGI BERRA

"Just take the ball and throw it where you want to. Throw strikes. Home plate don't move."

—SATCHEL PAIGE

"Don't look back. Something might be gaining on you."

—SATCHEL PAIGE

"I think about the cosmic snowball theory. A few million years from now the sun will burn out and lose its gravitational pull. The earth will turn into a giant snowball and be hurled through space. When that happens it won't matter if I get this guy out."

—BILL LEE

"I ain't never had a job, I just always played baseball."

—SATCHEL PAIGE

"In combat, spontaneity rules; rote performance of technique perishes."
—BRUCE LEE

"The height of cultivation always runs to simplicity."
—BRUCE LEE

"When Steve and I die, we are going to be buried in the same cemetery, 602†63†apart."
—TIM MCCARVER, WHO CAUGHT ALL STEVE CARLTON'S GAMES

"We catchers don't want the credit, and we don't want the blame. I've never called for a hanging curveball in my life."
—DAVID ROSS

"Most people don't understand catchers. For example, Jerry Grote is a catcher who hits. Johnny Bench is a hitter who catches. There is a big difference."
—JOE TORRE

"There are a lot more important things in life than baseball. I just haven't found out what they are yet."
—MARTY SCHUPAK

"Slumps are like a soft bed. They're easy to get into and hard to get out of."
—JOHNNY BENCH

"How many games was it before they told you about the mask?"
—HANK GREENWALD, SPORTSCASTER, TO ONETIME CATCHER KEN DITO

"My motto was always to keep swinging. Whether I was in a slump or feeling badly or having trouble off the field, the only thing to do was keep swinging."
—HANK AARON

"God was never a catcher because, if He was, there would never have been a knuckleball pitcher."
—CAPTAIN JACK KIRBY

Acknowledgments

I would like to acknowledge all of the coaches and managers I ever played for: Thank you for your time and service. I learned something from all of you without exception. Special thanks to Larry Corrigan for his forward thinking and making me feel like I was better than I was. Thanks to Jamie Nelson and Kirk Bauermeister for the younger years, John Mizerock for the K.C. years, and Jeff Cox for his enthusiasm. Thank you to Dennis Rogers for teaching me the foundation of a strong mental game. I would also like to recognize all of the players who came before me and all of my teammates over the years.

As far as this book goes, I could not have done it without a lot of help and guidance. Thank you to my friend and photography pro Mitch Haddad, who so kindly lent his services. Thank you to Chuck Rosciam and his great website, www.baseballcatchers. com. I'm very grateful to Ron Modra and Steve Dewing for letting me rummage through their vast collection of baseball images and to Scott Andrews, who provided me with a great logo design and drawing. Thank you to Andrew Newman and the folks at the National Baseball Hall of Fame for being so generous and helpful with their property. To Mark Langill and the Los Angeles Dodgers, thanks for the photos.

A big thank you to the gang at About Books for their guidance, patience, and hard work in making this book a reality.

Thank you to my wife Hillary and children, Dylan, Noah, and Jaya, for supporting me while I dragged you all over the country. Most of all, thank you to my mom Patricia and father Mike Mayne for teaching me the game of baseball and passing on the importance of focus, purpose, and always competing to the best of one's ability.

Index

Page numbers for illustrations are in italics.

Photo Credits

Catcher stance and position photos on pages 19, 20, 25, 27, 28, 29, 34, 36, 37, 38, 43, 44, 45, 52, 54, 55, 56, 75, 76, and 81: Mitch Haddad

Page 12:
photos of baseball Hall of Famers: National Baseball Hall of Fame Library, Cooperstown, NY

Page 13:
catcher's mitt photos: Chuck Rosciam, *www.baseballcatchers.com*

Page 14:
photos of Bresnahan and Schwert: Library of Congress

Page 14:
photos of Bench, Carter, and Fisk: National Baseball Hall of Fame Library, Cooperstown, NY

Page 15:
Mayne father and son photo: *Daily Pilot*

Page 18:
Ryan: Ron Modra
Sumo wrestler: Julian Tanioka
Surfer Burrow: Getty Images
Golfer Hogan: Getty Images/John Dominis
Rodriguez: National Baseball Hall of Fame Library

Page 19:
Bench-era catcher: Steve Dewing

Page 28:
Pena: Getty Images/B. Bennett

Page 35:
Mayne/KC photo: Michael Ponzini

Page 39:
Murcer "chicken-winging" photo: Steve Dewing

Page 50:
Thurman Munson photo: National Baseball Hall of Fame Library, Cooperstown, NY

Page 51:
Catcher position photos: Mitch Haddad
Yogi Berra/Ted Williams photo:
National Baseball Hall of Fame Library, Cooperstown, NY

Page 53:
Tom Seaver photo: Ron Modra

Page 57:
photos of Mike Scioscia and Ernie Lombardi: National Baseball Hall of Fame Library, Cooperstown, NY

Page 58:
Ivan Rodriguez photo: Ron Modra

Page 63:
Driefort and Mayne: Los Angeles Dodgers

Page 66:
Gagne and Mayne: Los Angeles Dodgers

Page 70:
drawing: Scott Andrews

Page 71:
Bench pop fly: National Baseball Hall of Fame Library, Cooperstown, NY
Cochrane pop fly: National Baseball Hall of Fame Library, Cooperstown, NY

Page 73:
Harnett play at the plate photo: National Baseball Hall of Fame Library, Cooperstown, NY

Page 74:
Cochrane photo: National Baseball Hall of Fame Library, Cooperstown, NY

Page 76:
Rick Ferrell photo: National Baseball Hall of Fame Library, Cooperstown, NY
Mike Sciocsia photo: Los Angeles Dodgers

Page 77:
Pat Borders/George Brett photo: Ron Modra

PHOTO SECTION (Pages 91-94):

Mickey Cochrane: National Baseball Hall of Fame Library, Cooperstown, NY

Yeager/Parker photo: Steve Dewing

Boone/Buckner photo: Steve Dewing

Robinson photo: Steve Dewing

Collins photo: Steve Dewing

Aaron photo: Steve Dewing

Henderson photo: Ron Modra

Mayne/Reilly photo: AP Images/Ed Zurga

Mayne crash photo (top): AP Images/Ed Zurga

Mayne crash photo (middle): AP Images/Mark J. Terrill

Mayne crash photo (bottom): AP Images/Nam Y. Huh

About the Author

Brent Mayne was a major-league catcher from 1989 to 2004. He played most of his career for the Kansas City Royals but also spent time with the New York Mets, Oakland A's, San Francisco Giants, Colorado Rockies, Arizona Diamondbacks, and Los Angeles Dodgers. He ranks 75th in the history of baseball with 1,143 pro games caught, and has the distinction of being the only catcher in the twentieth century to have won a game as a pitcher. An All-American in college, he was drafted in the first round and inducted into the Orange Coast College Hall of Fame in 2006. In his retirement, Brent has gone on to serve on the board of directors for both the Braille Institute and the Center for Hope and Healing. He enjoys surfing, fly fishing, golf, yoga, and traveling. Brent lives in California with his wife Hillary; they have three children.

Brent Mayne's website, **www.brentmayne.com**, has more helpful information for catchers, including video clips. Brent is also available for speaking engagements. Call 949-887-3355, or email bdanem@mac.com.

Made in the USA
Middletown, DE
21 August 2017